courage to surrender

courage to surrender

8 Contradictions on the Spiritual Path

TOMMY HELLSTEN

Translated and adapted from Finnish
by Timo Luhtanen

CELESTIAL ARTS
Berkeley | Toronto

This work was first published in Finnish by Kirjapaja, Helsinki, under the title *Saat sen mistä luovut*, copyright © 2000 by Tommy Hellsten and Kirjapaja Oy. English translation copyright © 2008 by Tommy Hellsten and Timo Luhtanen.

All rights reserved. No part of this book may be reproduced in any form, except brief excerpts for the purpose of review, without written permission of the publisher.

Celestial Arts
an imprint of Ten Speed Press
PO Box 7123
Berkeley, California 94707
www.tenspeed.com

Distributed in Canada
by Ten Speed Press Canada.

Book design by Katy Brown

Portions of this English-language edition have been adapted from other works by Tommy Hellsten and are used with permission from their respective Finnish publishers. These works include *Lähelle on pitkä matka* by Tommy and Carita Hellsten (Kirjapaja, 2004); *Kolme matkamiestä* by Tommy Hellsten (WSOY, 2006); and *Är det försent att förändras?* by Tommy Hellsten (Fontana Media, 2006).

"The Clearing" (excerpt) by Tomas Tranströmer, translated by Robin Fulton, from *The Great Enigma*, © 2006 by Tomas Tranströmer. Translation © 2006 by Robin Fulton. Reprinted by permission of New Directions Publishing Corp.

Scripture taken from the *Holy Bible: New International Version*®. Copyright © 1973, 1978, 1984 International Bible Society. Used by permission of Zondervan. All rights reserved. The "NIV" and "New International Version" trademarks are registered in the United States Patent and Trademark Office by International Bible Society. Use of either trademark requires the permission of International Bible Society.

Library of Congress Cataloging-in-Publication Data

Hellsten, Tommy.
  [Saat sen mistä luovut. English]
  Courage to surrender : eight contradictions on the spiritual path / Tommy Hellsten ; translated and adapted from the Finnish by Timo Luhtanen.
      p. cm.
  Summary: "An inspirational guide that explores eight seemingly paradoxical lessons on the road to personal growth, recovery, and spiritual development"—Provided by publisher.
  Includes index.
  ISBN-13: 978-1-58761-320-3
  ISBN-10: 1-58761-320-4
  1. Spiritual life. 2. Conduct of life. I. Title.
  BL624.H3835 2008
  248.4—dc22

                               2007039828

First printing, 2008
Printed in the United States of America

1 2 3 4 5 6 7 8 9 10 — 12 11 10 09 08

contents

acknowledgments	vi
to the reader	viii
introduction: sick with strength	1
1 ▪ the journey begins when you stop	9
2 ▪ true strength can only be found in weakness	16
3 ▪ if you seek safety, live dangerously	31
4 ▪ what you give up will be given to you	60
5 ▪ the less you do, the more you get done	83
6 ▪ only alone can we be together	109
7 ▪ only together can we be alone	124
8 ▪ if you seek eternity, live in the here and now	136
index	145
about the author	150

acknowledgments

I wrote the original version of this book amid the deepest crisis of my life: after twenty-five years, I had left a marriage that appeared perfect but was devoid of love. I wrote this book in a rental apartment furnished with only a bed, a kitchen table, and a few chairs. *What you give up will be given to you* was one of my essential messages, and I was a guinea pig for my own writing. I had become a public figure, and my credibility and career were at stake. I had risked everything to find out whether life carries us when we decide to do what we know to be right in our innermost being, even though this decision may seem unreasonable, dangerous, or outright insane. When the situation was at its worst, I felt that only a single brain cell in me believed that I had done the right thing; after all, I had also caused my wife, my children, and many others the greatest crises of their lives.

That was eight years ago. I know now that the divorce was the best thing that could have happened to us. Today, my children thank me for my courage; in their opinion, we should have divorced earlier. Today, I would like to thank everyone who supported me when I deserved their support the least but needed it the most. I was broken, and my life was shattered, but friends and relatives never ceased to believe in me. Without their encouragement, I would never have been able to finish this book.

I extend my warmest thanks to Carita, who never left my side throughout circumstances in which many would not have hesitated to abandon me. She later became my beloved wife.

I would also like to thank translator Timo Luhtanen from the bottom of my heart for making one of my greatest dreams come true. Without his professionalism and persistence, this book would never have found a home in the dauntingly competitive North American market.

Timo would like to thank editor Kristi Hein and copyeditor Nina K. Pettis for years of inspiring cooperation and friendship, and copyeditor Shirley Coe for adding the final touches to the manuscript on behalf of the publisher.

Our sincerest thanks to Elizabeth Evans and Kimberley Cameron at the Reece Halsey North literary agency; Whitney Lee at the Fielding Agency; and Jo Ann Deck, Julie Bennett, and Brie Mazurek at Celestial Arts. This North American edition could not have found a better home.

to the reader

When I set out to write this book, I did not realize that it would become a summary and a synthesis of all my previous books. I wrote my first book eighteen years ago, and it has taken me all these years to gain a deep understanding of the topics discussed in this book.

I have been going through an intense process of personal growth, chiefly exploring the connection between what I have discovered in my work as a therapist and what the Judeo-Christian tradition has known and taught about humanity for thousands of years. When I set out on this journey in the late 1970s, I was frustrated with the Christian church and its traditional teachings about life and humanity. I felt that they had given me no help at a time of great personal distress. So I abandoned faith and spirituality and turned inward, confronting the personal past that I had always feared and avoided. I set out to face my pain, my grief, and everything I had left behind in my childhood.

On my journey, I began to run into what I had abandoned: spirituality and faith. And now, to my surprise, spirituality resonated with me. Gradually I came to understand that when I had sought help from faith in the past, I had actually been running away from myself. I had used faith and spirituality as a refuge, hoping to avoid confronting all the things that I feared within. In other words, I had tried to leap into God's lap and close my eyes to reality. Fortunately, my pain had become so acute that even faith could not shield me from it.

When I chose the road to self-discovery, I thought that I had abandoned God. However, all I had really abandoned was my own misperception of God. In confronting myself, I also came face to face with reality. Reality is within me—and God lives there. When I realized this, my faith became more firmly grounded.

This book is a modest attempt to describe what this discovery means—to give voice to our spiritual inheritance, using the language in which these ancient truths have been slowly unfolding to me. I invite you to join the process in which I have been involved for more than thirty years. It is a journey that can open our eyes to the enormous richness of the Christian faith.

Our culture has hidden this richness behind religious dogma and sanctimonious language. So I extend an invitation in particular to readers who feel resentment toward Christian concepts and proclamations—those for whom, for this reason, the true richness of these teachings remains out of reach. I have tried to express these truths in my own words without distorting the essential message.

As humans, we can find our true lives and identities only after we become aware that Somebody loves us. We cannot find this miracle of love until we admit our weakness and powerlessness. There are no shortcuts. We can acquire strength only through weakness. This is why I write about paradox. The essence of Christianity is characterized by paradox. It is the small gate, the narrow road, that leads to life.

I hope you will take your time reading this book. It is not important that this book is read. It is important that this book reads you.

—Tommy Hellsten

INTRODUCTION
sick with strength

Everything seemed perfect at first. A handsome young man with a wave of fair hair falling over his forehead. A dark-haired beauty admired by every boy. I think my father took pride in winning the heart of the most beautiful girl in town. Perhaps my mother, at nineteen, also felt proud of having impressed the blond guitar player of a dance band, a man with a wistful smile and longing eyes. Life was full of promise.

Then this young beauty became pregnant. On a summer night, she surrendered to those pensive eyes, and suddenly everything changed: their romance turned into a tragedy, entrapping them both. The girl still wanted to live out her youth, feeling carefree, conquering hearts, and delighting in her beauty. But too early, too soon, life took them in its grip.

The girl's mother was known to be strict, so confiding in her about the baby was out of the question. The young man and the woman decided to marry, quickly, before anyone might suspect anything.

My arrival in this world was an accident, a stunning and shameful consequence of their summer bliss. I know this because my father once touched on the subject in conversation—and then proceeded to talk about his memories from the army, leaving me stupefied with the news.

But in spite of everything, the newlyweds built themselves a beautiful home and rejoiced in their newborn. I later learned that my grandmother had hastened to proudly present her grandson to the neighbors. My father was a photographer, and hundreds of pictures show my parents spending time with me, taking delight in their baby boy. In our old home movies I see scenes of what appears to be an ideal family of the fifties: my father, tall and handsome, wearing a tie and a gray fedora; my mother, a charming and, by all appearances, fashion-conscious young woman with a baby carriage. Both of them seem well and happy.

Their relationship, however, was a time bomb—they lacked what they needed to make the transition from falling in love to being in love. My mother was so young that she simply could not give up the pleasure of making heads turn; she relished her allure and used it to her advantage. My father grew jealous and took to drinking, and they argued more and more often, unable to recapture the state of falling in love. Father may have used alcohol socially and moderately at first, but in a few years his drinking was out of control. He may also have been retaliating against my mother for her flirtations. Gradually, the man of the family ceased to exist.

My parents ran a small but successful business that my father had established before meeting my mother. When he was caught, for the first time, driving under the influence and was sentenced to prison for three months, she took on more responsibility, and her position in both the business and the family became stronger.

His significance dwindled, which made him drink even more—but even though constantly drunk, he was always at work, and the entire town soon knew about his problem. Though we were confident that our secret was safe, we were actually well known as the alcoholic family.

My father stayed drunk for twenty years, with two exceptions: when he was sentenced for driving under the influence and when he was committed to treatment.

I picture my childhood family as a home in which no one is present—my father and mother were there physically, but not emotionally. My parents were occupied with their anguish and unfulfilled needs to such a degree that they had nothing to give to their children; after all, you cannot give what you do not have. They needed help; however, no one in our family would ever ask for help. What mattered most was keeping up the facade that all was well: everything had to *look* good because nothing *was* good. The shame had to be concealed at all costs. I remember once, at fourteen, when I was in a movie theater waiting for the show to begin, a group of men sitting behind me began to talk about the blunders of some stupid alcoholic. I was mortified when I realized they were talking about my father.

Over the years, shame became a member of our family. We never talked about this new member; we never showed the grief, anger, and embarrassment it caused us. I could not see my own loneliness, sorrow, and shame, because no one else saw them. I even learned to hide behind wisecracks about my father's drinking. We adapted ourselves to the shame, and it became part of our everyday life, requiring more and more space. It was as though a hippo had suddenly moved into our living room. This image captures both the magnitude and the cruel absurdity of shame—we needed to go to ever-greater lengths to pretend it was not there.

Shame flourishes wherever love loses ground. In my family, we were each isolated from the others within the same four walls, unable to reveal our innermost selves to each other. We lost contact, communication, communion. And so our personalities became bound with shame, which also laid the foundation for my identity. My needs and feelings were rooted in shame.

I had lost my father to alcoholism, my mother had lost her husband, and she was soon to vanish herself, as she had to bear all the responsibility of running a family. She grew strong, but her strength was based on a denial of weakness; in other words, she became sick with strength. At the same time, she instinctively sought support and consolation, and she discovered me, her oldest child. She began to confide in me, converse with me, need me. She no longer saw me as a child; she saw me only through her unfulfilled needs. My childhood ended, and I became sick with the same strength.

What was left was a family without parents, in which each member had to survive by whatever means he or she could find. My mother and I became allies; together we derided my father—which was fairly easy, because his behavior did not exactly command respect. My role in the family was to emotionally compensate my mother for the lack of a husband. I was alert and attuned to the needs of others. I consoled my mother and listened to her, then discussed with my father whatever she wanted to convey to him.

The only peaceful place in our house was the boiler room. There I ran my first practice. With the central heating system humming softly in the background, I engaged in what I believed to be profound discussions with my father or mother; my purpose was to help my father quit drinking and save the marriage. In that boiler room I became the family counselor on call. Ironically, my father used to hide his bottles in the same room; the more problems he reported with the heating, the more drunk he would become.

My work as a counselor was based on the wisdom and experience of a fifteen-year-old. Once, when my aunt asked me what I wanted to be when I grew up, I told her I wanted to become a psychiatrist. In reality, I was one already. I brought hosts of books home from the library and tried to study Freud, Erich Fromm, and the like, although I did not understand much of it—after all, this was professional literature. I also acquainted myself with Chinese philosophy, with the guidance of Lin Yutang. (I remember reading that in the morning you should let your toes rest peacefully on a hair carpet before you head out to meet the challenges of the new day.)

When I was seventeen, my parents reached an inevitable conclusion: they began to contemplate divorce. In those days, divorce was an even more complicated issue than it is today (if that is possible), so my parents sought my advice. Did I think they should divorce? I remember replying, after careful thought, that they should—and they did, within six months. The issue of alcoholism was never addressed. Quite the contrary; after the family fell apart, my mother also became an alcoholic. Ten years after the divorce, she committed suicide.

After my family exploded into pieces, wherever I landed I began to help others, because that was the role I had learned to adopt at home. At nineteen, after completing my military service, I began my studies, thinking that I would finally achieve freedom.

I eventually decided to major in theology, but found myself working as an alcohol abuse counselor in the late seventies. I had not yet realized that in my choice of career I was really fumbling for help for myself. Little did I know that I was carrying my disregarded childhood needs inside—unresolved, and thus as compelling as ever.

Through my work, I came into contact with the Minnesota Model for addiction treatment, as well as the 12-step program. And when I encountered the support movement for adult children of alcoholics—then a new phenomenon—I felt as though I had finally come home. This initiated a powerful inner process, which turned into a journey into my past, to the origin of my wounds and hurt, to my true identity. Until then I had always been only what others had needed, but through this process I was born as who I am.

Emotional pain is not an incurable disease, but in my case, recovering from childhood took years of hard work. Having acted as a family therapist of sorts from my early teens, I had gradually lost sight of my real self, defining myself in terms of what others needed from me. I was not allowed to need or trust anyone or to be weak, and this survival strategy prevented me from facing all the pain I had experienced. Only in adulthood did I begin to realize how this had affected me. I sensed that this pain was an obstacle to a good life, an obstacle I would have to dismantle.

I mustered the courage to look myself in the eye in the mirror—and there was no one there. I realized that, even though I was now over thirty, I had never lived. I had merely survived. Bit by bit, behind my childhood pains, I began to discern what I had been looking for: my own identity. In my family of origin, I had never been seen as the person I really was, so I had grown up to be someone else. Behind that someone was a person whose existence no one had witnessed; a person burdened with grief, fear, and insecurity; a person who'd had to assume too great a responsibility at too early an age. I also discovered plenty of anger without an outlet and a great deal of loneliness.

With the help of lengthy therapy, self-help groups, and psychodrama, my personality finally resurfaced through my ingrained sense of shame. I realized that I was not a bad person; I had spent my whole life *feeling* bad, and thus had lost my entire childhood and beyond.

I found the help I sought through my choice of career, but I did not abandon my work as a therapist. No longer working to gain an identity, I now worked because I finally had one and could see others more clearly through my own experience, the process through which I had reconnected with my true identity.

During this process, I also began to write books—as of today I have written seventeen. In addition, for twenty years now I have given lectures and workshops in different countries. I have also run a private practice—no longer in a boiler room—for seventeen years, meeting hundreds and hundreds of people like myself, people who have lost their childhoods and harbored immense shame. I have been blessed with the honor of sharing their journeys as a guide and traveling companion.

This book has been a best seller in my home country, as was my first, *Hippo in the Living Room*—and I cannot even begin to describe my surprise at this. After my first book was published, I soon found myself referred to as "the national therapist," and I had to become a public person, which is not easy for a person who was once bound with shame. But I have endured and even learned to enjoy it, and publicity has become part of my work, even though I always liked to think I was only writing about my own life. I now realize that all along I must have also been writing and speaking about a common experience: about the wounds that we recognize in ourselves and others, but also about the great joy we share on our journeys of discovery.

I am happy to say that today I feel good. I am married, for the second time, and have three wonderful children from my first marriage. My oldest son has recently joined my wife and me in our family business to continue my life's work, and my two other children seem to be following in his footsteps. The journey has been long, but what once was my greatest weakness seems to have turned into my greatest strength. I have my weakness to thank for everything; weakness has been my greatest treasure and blessing.

This is why I write so much about weakness. This is why I write that true strength begins with acknowledging weakness; we are able to grow only to the extent that we are willing to embrace our weakness. In fact, true growth means that we actually become smaller, more profoundly aware of our powerlessness. Humility is essential to this growth. When we face our weakness, we also realize that we cannot survive alone: we need one another; we need communion. Weakness opens us to love, to what we need the most as human beings. And when we need love, we need God, who loves us not in spite of our weakness, but because of our weakness. God is the love that always respects our innermost self. God is the love that creates each of us as a unique being.

CHAPTER 1

the journey begins when you stop

As someone else wisely put it, life is to be lived, not understood, and this rings true for me. First you must live; only then can you try to understand some small part of your experience. If you try to comprehend life instead of living it, you examine it intellectually from a safe distance, and your loss is twofold. First, when you rely solely on your intellect, you view life through a distorted glass—one that alters your perception and can lead you astray. Your intellect thus becomes an obstacle to living. Second, when you take refuge from life in your head instead of taking part, you remain a bystander, never getting your hands dirty.

In this life you are *supposed* to get dirt under your fingernails. You are supposed to break, get lost, and be confused. You should not use your intellect to regulate, apportion, or filter life. Life is a phenomenon much bigger than the human mind. Your intellect is your servant, not your master; it must find its place within a much greater context.

The intellect is not the best tool for solving life's great questions. Rather, it is a survival tool better suited for procuring your daily bread and butter. For this kind of practical coping, the intellect is in its element. But in the face of life's great mysteries—such as the questions of love, suffering, death, God, and identity, and the meaning of existence—you must allow your intellect to retreat gracefully into the background and remain silent. *Who am I and what should I make of you, life? What is the truth, the truth about life and myself?* We cannot answer these questions intellectually. We need other means, other tools, other approaches.

paradoxes are unreasonable

Life's deep wisdoms and truths are often paradoxical. They appear irrational and contradictory, as though life has declared itself a mystery that does not respect the laws of rational thinking and logic. Life often manifests itself as an absolute majesty that does not submit to control, not even by the human intellect that we so insistently revere as the most miraculous work of creation.

When truth is revealed in the form of a paradox, it creates a seeming contradiction, an impossibility. Jesus employed paradox in his teachings. In response to man's desire for greatness, he presented its exact opposite: servitude and modesty. He said, "The last will be first, and the first will be last," and then spoke of descending into greatness: "Whoever wants to become great among you must be your servant."

Jesus's teachings confused people. He disturbed and upset conventional ways of thinking. He disconcerted wise men and would not let himself be caught in doctrinal disputes. Refusing to quibble, he confronted the smug and self-satisfied with paradox.

A paradox is life's way of showing us that truth cannot be controlled. Though our intellect may fume with indignation when a paradox brings it to a halt, truth remains serenely unaffected. With supreme authority, truth manifests itself in opposites—and between opposites there is always tension. Life uses this tension to create something new.

We should rightly regard paradoxes with awe. A paradox stops us, enabling us to become still and receptive to a deepening of our experience. The tension generated by a paradox weakens our controlling intellect's grip. Thus we should not strive to understand a paradox; we should simply allow ourselves to listen to it. Listening, being, wondering, and humility are fruitful approaches to a paradox. "The wind blows wherever it pleases. You hear its sound, but you cannot tell where it comes from or where it is going." Jesus said this about the Holy Spirit, and it seems to apply to paradoxes as well: the wisdom of a paradox cannot be confined by reason.

A paradox works by stimulating self-doubt and self-questioning. Our intellect offers ready answers that seem to shelter us from the discomfort experienced when seeking the truth; with this false knowledge, our mind creates the illusion of complacency and contentment. A paradox offers no such safe haven. It sweeps you along on a journey that may be unpleasant, during which you may—or, perhaps, should—lose your way.

wisdom is intellect in a refined form

When our intellect encounters a paradoxical truth, it runs into its own limits. Bewildered and perplexed, it is no longer in control. If our intellect is willing to humble itself, it is transformed into wisdom. *Wisdom is intellect in a refined form—a humble form.*

When our intellect confronts a paradox, humility is the only right approach, for it leads to wisdom. When our intellect humbles itself in the face of a paradox, it finds its rightful place. It does not place itself above life and personal growth, but chooses collaboration. A wise person finds the right use for his intellect; conversely, the person who misuses his intellect is not very wise.

A humble person listens more than he talks—and so the humble learn faster than the proud. A proud person does not have time to listen; he is busy trying to convince others of his greatness. Because he does not listen, his mind is closed to new perspectives. When we are humble we have no need to impress others; we know who we are. We are free to listen—and to learn and discover new things. On the road to wisdom, we will inevitably gain the ability to listen.

true wisdom holds more questions than answers

Wisdom is more about questions than about answers. Paradoxes confuse us and raise questions, thus leading us to wisdom. Questions are dynamic; they keep pushing us into the unknown. Therefore, the wise person spends more time wondering than providing answers. Those who rush to provide answers think that they have already reached their destination, though their journey has not even begun. A wise person knows that he is on a journey that will last for a lifetime. He is constantly on the move, inspired by the wonders he meets on his way.

Paradoxes annoy those who are sure they have the answers. For those who are less sure, facing a paradox is an opportunity to enjoy a new level of learning, where wondering will take you further than clinging to established facts. On this level we must get lost in order to reach our destination. The Swedish poet Tomas Tranströmer put it beautifully: "Deep in the forest there's an unexpected clearing that can be reached only by someone who has lost his way."

Understanding a paradox requires this openness to getting lost—and for that, we need courage, for losing our way challenges us to embrace insecurity. When Jesus teaches his paradoxical truths, he invites us to relinquish our control of life. He is actually inviting us to safety—the eternal safety we can find only within ourselves. This courage to surrender requires a leap of faith. We must let go of our cherished safety structures, allow them to collapse, and trust that we will find security through insecurity.

when we stop, the journey begins

This book is a modest attempt to describe the old paradoxical wisdom of spirituality, which reflected life at the deepest level. Today, we have severed our connection with those who created this wisdom—created it when the need for it was still understood—and in so doing, we have lost our connection with our past. We have become a generation without depth, a generation that worships youth, oblivious to the value of those who have lived long. When we lose our connection to our past, we cut ourselves off from the wisdom therein.

We live only for the moment, as if each day were our last. We have relegated spirituality and the wisdom of the old to our museums. In order to live for the moment, always remaining young, we close our eyes to death as well. We have done our best to vanquish death: As long as life is entertaining and fun, it does not matter how we live our lives, for we feel as if we'll live forever. If life starts to feel empty, we busy ourselves looking for more entertainment—not realizing that in denying death we have also banished life's natural drama. We have redefined life as a shallow and empty existence. With death out of the picture, wisdom and life experience become useless. This is why we no longer understand the mysterious mutterings and rituals that were once called wisdom and spirituality.

The things I speak of are not new; they are old truths, well known by those who walked here before us—known not by all, but by many. This book is an invitation to a deeper life, in which everything is true and all is real. It is an invitation to discover the source of our true identity, where God is within us.

I have struggled for years with the timeworn old expressions: sin, mercy, "God loves you," holiness, sanctity, the soul, and so on. Like so many, I have been perplexed by these words. They have filled me with frustration, resentment, and rage, because even though I realize they contain something precious, they seemed to keep it to themselves. However, I have finally begun to catch a glimpse of what these words may mean. Just a glimpse, but enough for me to continue my journey of exploration and to share what I have learned with you.

Adventure awaits us in the depths of life. We can take part in this adventure only if we learn to slow down, calm down, and come to a full stop. The road to a meaningful life passes through standstill and silence—and here we are met by the first paradox of this book: *The journey begins when you stop.*

This book should not be read in one sitting. I hope you will take your time, stopping to listen, to find your own depth; each of us has our own inner sounding board for wisdom and depth. When the time is right, it will begin to resonate. It's my hope that the thoughts in this book will guide you to a slowing, a stilling, and finally such a complete standstill that a new kind of movement can begin: downward movement, deep down, so deep that you can reach stunning new heights. Perhaps with the help of this book you will begin to look inward, to an inner darkness that eventually dazzles with its brightness.

CHAPTER 2

true strength can only be found in weakness

The question of strength and weakness remains unresolved in our society. We do not quite know how to deal with weakness; we hide our own weakness and shun it in others, while admiring strength in its different forms and anxiously striving to acquire it for ourselves. We seek strength, for we think that only the strong get what they need, while the weak must settle for leftovers. Seeing no value in weakness, we have built a culture that strives for strength. And we do not just deny weakness—we often hold it in contempt.

But what is weakness, actually, and what is strength? The person who appears strong—is he really strong, or could it be that his strength is used to cover weakness? In other words, is there an unhealthy kind of strength? Is it possible to become sick with this strength? Is our culture catching this disease, as it loses touch with the value of weakness?

Are there superior strong people and inferior weak people—or are we all, in fact, weak? Or strong? What is normal, and what is not? Does weakness make a person bad or defective? Is strength defined by a lack of weakness, or does a denial of weakness lead to strength? Or could it be that true strength originates in weakness? Could it be that those who are in harmony with their weakness are strong?

What about weakness, then? Does it mean putting oneself down? Am I humble if I do not make an issue of myself? Is such humility a feature of which we can be aware? Is it possible to achieve humility by striving for it? Does it pay to be humble; in other words, is humility a "good deal," does it have market value, does it make us strong? And what is the difference between self-pity and honest acknowledgment of weakness—or is there a difference? Is it possible to hide behind weakness to avoid taking responsibility for one's own life and personal growth?

These questions perplex us, and they are part of our everyday life, even if we are not grappling with them consciously. Clearly, strength and weakness are opposites full of the dynamic tension characteristic of a paradox. Could this tension be a sign of the mysterious wisdom also found in a paradox? If we become aware of this wisdom, will it lead us to a deeper understanding of life and, therefore, to a deeper life?

humility: there is strength in weakness

This question of strength and weakness is one of the most important questions in life—if not the most important. It has to do with our essential identity, for this pair of opposites leads us to the question of our inner and outer selves. In a culture that finds weakness despicable and shameful, we feel that we must at least appear strong. We work hard to establish a facade of strength that hides our weakness. The greater the weakness we feel within, the more convincing our facade must be. We might well conclude, then, that the stronger a person appears, the greater the weakness he hides within. This kind of strength, developed to hide weakness, is not healthy, for it has no foundation in reality. When strength is all we communicate, we are not revealing our real selves. We are true and authentic only when we acknowledge our weakness, embrace it, and reveal it.

What might this weakness look like, then, if it were visible, if we revealed it? It is humility: *humility is strength that does not deny weakness*. In fact, true strength originates in weakness, for it requires owning up to weakness. *True strength, then, is humility, which results from facing and coming to terms with our weakness.* The humble person is real because he has discovered and acknowledged his powerlessness. Thus we meet the second paradox of this book: *True strength can only be found in weakness.*

If you look more closely at people who strive for wealth or power, in contrast, you will find that they are actually striving for a cover-up for their weakness. A person may strive for power in an effort to attain a position that feels secure and strong, far removed from weakness. Of course, power is not always an indication that the powerful person is fleeing from weakness, but it can be. The same is true of wealth: if a person amasses wealth and clings to material things, he eventually reaches a state of affluence that appears immune to weakness. Like power, wealth in itself is not necessarily a sign that a person is trying to hide his weakness, but it can be.

In our culture, outward impressions have become more important than our authentic selves—so important, in fact, that we often come to believe the surface identity that we present to others is our true identity. Most of us devote a lot of effort and energy to making a favorable impression on others. We try to dress in the latest fashions, patronize the right restaurants, and socialize with the right people. This effort may extend to decorating our house, going to the gym, losing weight, driving a certain kind of car, reading the right books, spending vacations in the right places, going shopping where the latest trends are created, and even enduring plastic surgery.

To charm and impress, we craft positive representations of ourselves: streamlined, polished versions stripped of such embarrassing flaws as clumsiness, uncertainty, and lack of style. We present these versions to convince ourselves and others that we have no weaknesses. Only when we have managed to convince everybody else that we are strong do we feel we have earned the right to live. However, we pay a heavy price for this charade. When we are not truthful, we cannot find true intimacy, and the lack of intimacy leads to loneliness.

love fosters weakness

The question of strength and weakness leads us straight to the question of love. We cannot afford to be weak unless we are surrounded by love. Without love, it is not safe to be weak. This is why we build our elaborate exteriors. The less we know of love, the stronger the facade we feel compelled to construct.

Love fosters weakness, allowing us to reveal our powerlessness. Love has such a deep respect for us that it embraces our authentic selves, letting us be who we really are. Love is not shocked or repelled by weakness; on the contrary, it makes room for it. In fact, love—like true strength—originates in weakness. We all know that it is difficult to love someone who is superficially strong and conceited. But it is easy to love someone who is weak, for this weakness awakens our sympathies. This is exactly why children engender our love. The weakness we see in them is natural—and in it, we recognize ourselves.

Of course, weakness can also arouse contempt. Those who are running away from their own weakness despise it in others. The more we deny the weakness within us, the greater our need to condemn others. This is the logic behind bullying at school and in the workplace. Bullies lack self-esteem; in other words, they lack the capacity to love themselves, so they try to bolster their self-image at the expense of others—to become a little bit taller by stepping on somebody else.

truth reveals false strength

The question of strength and weakness is also a question of truth, for truth reveals false strength. *Truth seeks to tear down our facades and reveal our authentic selves—to return us to reality.*

A person who has come to terms with his weakness has a strong sense of reality. As human beings, our reality encompasses our weakness. All humans are weak; there is no other kind. And so we find our true identity when we face our weakness. When we embrace our weakness, we realize that we cannot make it through life on our own. We begin to see that we must depend on others, and we begin allowing ourselves to feel that need. The more profound our understanding of this truth, the greater our understanding of the meaning of healthy dependency. Being dependent on others means, in fact, being dependent on love. Love creates the sheltering surroundings in which weakness can make itself at home. Love is the context in which we are meant to live our lives.

The humble person is a realist because he acknowledges his weakness. The person who seeks to cover up his weakness is anything but a realist. On the outside, he may appear mighty and convincing—so convincing that everybody believes he is what he appears to be. That is the purpose of his mightiness: to conceal his weakness behind a facade of strength, a masterpiece of illusion through which only the most perceptive can see. This illusion may be composed of such attributes as an impressive body of knowledge. The problem is not knowledge itself, but our attitude toward knowledge. Real knowledge is humble; it knows its own limits. As the saying goes, the more a person knows, the more he knows how little he knows.

The road to truth leads through weakness. There is no other way. Truth strives to lead us to our own powerlessness, weakness, and helplessness. If we are willing to acknowledge our weakness, truth will make us free. But it will also make us hurt. It is not easy to face something we have done our utmost to avoid. Therefore, we need love as well as truth in this encounter with our weakness. We cannot face the truth of our whole selves without love to shelter us from the inevitable hurt.

lack of love leads to shame

Love enables us to face our weakness; thus, love leads us to our true identity. There is probably nothing we need more than love. But, as we all can see, love often seems scarce in a world full of cruelty, war, exploitation, envy, and bitterness. We get very little of what we need the most. Even children are subjected to utmost cruelty and lack of love—children, who most need and deserve our love. This happens everywhere, even in homes that outwardly appear perfect.

This lack of love is not only apparent in the way we treat those closest to us; it also affects the way we treat ourselves. We often treat ourselves badly, even contemptuously. We abuse substances to feel good; we work unreasonably hard to gain acceptance; we overeat to smother our longing for love; we stop eating in an effort to lose weight and receive love; we torment ourselves at the gym in our effort to be good enough.

Lack of love is a fact in ourselves and in our world; it has always been and, apparently, will always be. Only those of us—far too many of us—who do not even know what love is can ignore this sad fact. So many of us have never been touched by love—and without knowing what we have missed, we cannot even grieve for the loss. Children who grow up without love never really have the childhood they were entitled to. To grieve for this loss, they must have the chance to experience, at least a little, what it feels like to be loved for who they are. Gaining this experience of love is one of the goals of therapy, or at least it should be.

Lack of love creates *shame—a sense of disgrace and unworthiness.* This happens to children who must adapt themselves to unresolved family issues, such as alcoholism, violence, sexual abuse, or rigid religious practices. When these issues are not addressed, children misinterpret their feelings, experiences, and perceptions. If it is forbidden to talk about the father's alcoholism, for example, the child cannot process his feelings, thoughts, or perceptions. Instead of connecting his anger, sadness, hurt, or fear with what is going on in the family, he perceives his own emotional responses as personal flaws. He thinks, "There must be something wrong with me. I must be a bad person." He does not realize that he is feeling bad because he is being treated badly. In this situation, the child's personality becomes entangled in shame. Everything within—hopes, fears, reactions, memories, feelings—is bound with shame. Shame becomes a normal state of being.

When we live with shame, our weakness feels like a flaw, and we believe that we are failures as human beings. Shame is like a hungry predator that lurks at love's heels. The instant that love falters and wanes, shame attacks. Shame steals away the protective love needed to shelter our natural human weakness. When love is not present, the sense of shame takes over. This does not necessarily require dramatic events or secrets in the family, such as alcoholism or sexual abuse—all it takes is the simple absence of love.

We are, in essence, dependent on love. To find our true identities, we must be seen, heard, and acknowledged as the people we really are. Here I am reminded of a magical moment in my own life, back in the early eighties, when my oldest son, Mathias, was three years old and we lived by the sea. It was a winter's night—the sea was frozen, and the sky was dotted with stars. I decided to take my son along for a walk on the frozen bay, where the night was darkest and the stars at their brightest. When we reached the middle of the bay, we decided to lie down on our backs on

true strength can only be found in weakness

the ice to better see the brilliant stars, thousands of them; the sky appeared low, almost within our reach. Right there it occurred to me that I should ask my son how he felt about all this, how he perceived the world we live in. So I asked, "What do you think, Mathias; who has made all the stars?" He paused to think for a moment, then replied with the innocence and sincerity of a child: "Daddy!"

That was one of the greatest moments of my life—not because my son thought so highly of his father, but because his response told me something essential about the world of a child. My son felt that his father had created the universe in which we live, and the child felt very special: he was the child of the Starmaker.

If the Starmaker spends time with his child—takes an interest in him, listens to him, and takes him seriously—it must mean that the child is very special, important, and lovable. The child senses this attitude, and over time he internalizes it as his own perception of his personal value. This is one way self-respect is woven into a budding personality. If the Starmaker does not take his child seriously, but instead belittles, mocks, and rejects him, the child will read his limited value in this lack of love. Thus the child, when subjected to a parent's abuse and abandonment, does not conclude that the parent is thoughtless, cruel, unfair; rather, he draws conclusions about his own unworthiness. An abandoned child learns to abandon himself; a loved one learns to love himself. We need someone who loves us and is there for us, for we do, to a great extent, treat ourselves just as we have been treated—picking up where our parents and other important people in our lives left off. Any lovelessness we experienced in the past carries over into our attitude toward ourselves. And if we are unable to embrace our imperfection, we try to conceal it.

When our identities are based in shame, we strive to build ever more elaborate facades to convince others that we are admirable and worthy. We may compulsively help others, become "workaholics," act overly nice and polite, clown around to get attention, or take unnecessary risks to appear heroic. All these efforts have one thing in common: they isolate us from others. In our shame, we cannot safely share our weakness with others. We avoid true intimacy in every possible way, because it could reveal our weakness.

Being in a constant hurry is one way of avoiding closeness. If we keep ourselves busy, we can keep our encounters with other people safely superficial. To do so, we must convince ourselves that external circumstances force us into this constant rush. We refuse to admit that we create all this hurry and worry ourselves. Yet it is a result of poor choices; it exists only because we want it to exist, for it serves an important purpose in our life. This is a truth that a person with a shame-based identity does not want to hear. If he did, he would have to face his weakness and take responsibility for his choices.

hope lies not in strength, but in weakness

The Alcoholics Anonymous 12-step recovery program has become firmly established in Western culture. A broad range of groups—including drug addicts, adult children of alcoholics, overeaters, sex addicts, and survivors of sexual abuse—are applying it to a variety of problems.

The 12-step program was established by a group of alcoholics who decided to write down some of the principles that had helped them achieve sobriety after years of alcoholic hell. This gave the program a solid foundation. It is a practical program, encouraging changes in behavior, not in religious beliefs. The program offers spiritual and psychological wisdom originating from the Judeo-Christian tradition, but does not require members to affiliate with any religious tradition or doctrine.

The 12-step program is spiritual in a deep and healthy way. From the very first step, the program addresses the issue of weakness: "We admitted that our lives had become unmanageable and that we were powerless over alcohol." Each person admits that he cannot make it on his own. His hope lies not in his strength, but in his weakness; when he acknowledges this, his growth begins. This program guides the alcoholic not only to sobriety, but also to personal and spiritual growth, in other words, to the origins of true strength. This strength can be harnessed only by those who are willing to face their weakness with courage and honesty.

Before reaching this step, the alcoholic has probably tried to fight his drinking habit on his own for years or even decades. He has tried to be strong and control his drinking in many ways: he has made promises of sobriety; he has moved to another city; he has sworn to stick to "light" alcoholic drinks; he has married and started a family; he has changed jobs, found new buddies, launched a demanding exercise routine, stopped traveling. He has tried everything he can think of to be strong and in control of his drinking.

But nothing has stopped him from drinking. He can stop only after he has realized that he cannot stop. This paradox is difficult for him to understand until he realizes the immense power inherent in acknowledging weakness. Even now, his efforts are useless.

He does not stop drinking; instead, alcohol becomes useless in his life as long as he stays in touch with his weakness. For this reason, it is important that he still refer to himself as an alcoholic in 12-step program meetings. He continues to do so even after years or decades of sobriety. He is a sober alcoholic. This is his way of saying, mainly to himself, that his sobriety and growth depend on his staying attuned to his weakness.

The 12-step program has uncovered a truth that applies to all human life: we can grow only to the extent that we acknowledge our need for growth. Jesus said that it is not the healthy who need to be healed, it is the sick. He did not mean that there are perfect people who have no need to grow and change, and then there are all the rest of us who do; he meant that a core prerequisite for growth is the acknowledgment of sickness. This creates the need to heal. A healthy awareness of sickness is the first harbinger of health.

This development is about humility—about admitting and accepting our weakness. We humans, however, feel compelled to hide our weakness—not only from others, but from ourselves. We deny our sickness and incompleteness, unaware that weakness is an essential part of human life. Because we do not truly love ourselves, we regard our weakness as a flaw and a sign of failure, so we try to make ourselves seem better than we actually are—to seem "normal." Once we have managed to convince ourselves that we are normal, we leave it at that. We feel no need to grow or examine ourselves; instead, we examine others. We find faults and shortcomings; we are absolutely certain that others should grow and change. We earnestly give them advice on changing the error of their ways, and we prove our noble nature by offering to help them in their hour of need. This is nothing more than ordinary pride, but pride in such a sophisticated form that it often goes unnoticed.

in weakness we learn what is valuable in life

What is the true value of weakness? What is this powerlessness that we need to acknowledge in order to grow? Does it truly exist?

In our Western culture, most of us manage the job of life quite well. On the surface, we appear neither powerless nor weak. We have it made, more or less: we do our jobs, have plenty to eat, have some free time to enjoy; we buy stocks, raise children, surf the Internet, hold strategy meetings. So why all this talk about weakness and powerlessness? What does it have to do with us? Why should we, all of a sudden, develop these strange qualities when our lives seem to be going along just fine?

Superficially, powerlessness seems remote. Despite the conflict, violence, and suffering that plague so much of humanity—to which no nation is now immune—life in the First World is still relatively safe and secure, compared to the rest of the globe. Here, most people's basic needs are met, and beyond that many enjoy an embarrassment of consumer goods and comforts.

But on closer examination, under the surface we are not doing well at all. The gloss and trappings of the good life cover up sadness and anger, bitterness and hurt. Most of us harbor an unmet need for closeness with others. In many of us, this longing to be loved manifests itself as a gnawing pain that wakes us each morning and troubles our sleep each night.

We often dwell on painful questions about the meaning of life: Who am I and what am I living for? Why do I force myself to wake up every morning and go to a job that I do not love? Why am I constantly worried and sad? Why am I afraid of the future, illness, poverty, death? Do I have to spend the rest of my life alone? Why do I feel so lonely even though I wake up beside someone every morning? Am I condemned to be with this person just because I lack the courage to leave? Why don't I ever seem to have enough money? Why don't my children respect me? Why do I always wake up with a headache? Why does my stomach always hurt? Why don't I ever seem to have any spare time? Why do work problems wake me up in the middle of the night? Why hasn't life changed for the better?

Where do these questions come from? What do they mean? Are they extraneous disturbances that unfairly sabotage our happiness—intruders to be silenced as irrelevant and inconsequential? Or do we need to pay serious attention to these messages? Could it be that these questions result from our inability to face weakness? Do they come from the place in which we secretly harbor feelings of neglect and rejection? If we try, all our lives, to avoid something of essential importance within us, this suppressed part of us will eventually surface with such intensity that it shakes the fortifications we have built to protect our hollow happiness.

As far as I can see, these questions arise from deep within us, from our true identity. With annoying persistence, they keep knocking at the door because they carry essential messages about all that we have overlooked and abandoned in ourselves and our lives. They come from the land of weakness. They are envoys from the place to which we are headed.

But where are we headed? Does anyone still know the direction of life?

Of one thing, at least, we can be sure: for each of us, life in its familiar form will one day come to an end. We are headed toward the moment when we open our hands and life slips away. Death is the ultimate weakness. It means total loss of control over our lives—total helplessness and surrender.

Could it be that this loss of control awaiting us at the end of our days is an indication of what is important in life? Perhaps life invites us to relinquish control before it is taken from us, irrevocably, by death. The reality of death hints at the value of the life that precedes it. Death reminds us to live our lives well and consider what is truly important. Because death will strip us of everything that is unnecessary, it offers a baseline for our lives. Whatever does not endure in the face of death is not, in the end, important. In this sense, death can be seen as the culmination of human life. It is the victorious fanfare that ends the lifelong process of growth. It is our most joyous award ceremony—and our award is our entry into something new at the end of our old existence.

We are headed toward utter weakness. But *in weakness we learn what is valuable and enduring in life*. In acknowledging our weakness, we enter life through death. Our facades collapse, our false selves die, and we are reunited with our true and authentic selves.

CHAPTER 3

if you seek safety, live dangerously

In our Western culture we have built a society that is safer than many others. We have been able to nearly eradicate hunger, thirst, war, and cold. We have eliminated encounters with death and suffering from our everyday life—just a few generations removed from a time when people normally suffered and died at home. Although we have not gained control over death, we have managed to create circumstances that keep death as far as possible from our daily existence. Through the ages people increasingly have sought their way to large cities, retreating from natural catastrophes and insecurity. Though nature is beyond our command, in cities we feel safely distanced from these occurrences, living in an artificial world under the delusion of almost perfect control.

In eliminating all natural drama from our society, we are easily lulled into the notion that life itself can be controlled. We begin to think and believe that life cannot—and should not—touch or hurt us. We place ourselves above the majesty of life's natural processes, dictating conditions and making demands. This is tragic, because in so doing we lose our lives: our existence may appear secure and fully under our control, but life itself is no longer present. However, life cannot be tricked, and it refuses to be observed from a safe distance. Life offers no secure positions and consequently no way of avoiding wounds, bruises, and dirt marks—on the contrary, only by enduring the pain of misfortune can we truly savor the triumphant joys of life. These belong together; we cannot have one without the other.

changing from a water animal to a conscious life

Life is a journey in which the eventual purpose is the journey itself, the continuous process of death and birth. Naturally, we reach a destination every once in a while, but only for a moment—after a short rest, we must continue into a new unknown. This course is set in the very first moments of life.

We enter this life as a water animal of sorts, floating in the womb. Newly developing, we rest in a safe, fluid-filled space that seems infinite; we are blissfully unaware of what lies ahead. Gradually, we must abandon our first state of existence and grow into a mammal, only to be violently wrenched away from our secure watery universe. An arduous journey begins—the passage through the nearly lethal embrace of the birth canal into an unknown world. There is no time to look back and long for lost safety, no time to mourn the end of an entire world. We emerge into a bright and noisy place where everything is new and different. This unknown is our new world, and the comforting fluid is replaced with air, which penetrates our lungs with explosive force, triggering a rhythmic movement that will later gain a name: *breathing*. All this marks the beginning of our new existence as a horizontal mammal surrounded by aimlessly moving things that occasionally hit us in the face; we will later realize these are part of us: our hands. And we notice moving things of another kind, which are harder to understand. These do not hit us in the face, but they clearly have something to do with us: our legs. Their purpose remains unclear at this stage but is revealed later, as we must learn to place our entire weight on them and then move from one place to another in the new and strange world. So after all these upheavals, we have not reached our destination; instead, we soon have no choice but to abandon our horizontal world and head toward bewildering new discoveries.

Somewhere along our journey in this new world, we realize that we are not alone. We detect another—gradually, this proves to be a creature called "Mother." Mother seems to come and go as she pleases, but we notice that the sounds coming from our throat have an effect on her. With time, we also notice that we are not the only reason for Mother's existence; she has an entire world of her own. These two universes begin to communicate, creating something called a consciousness. Expelled from our watery paradise, we develop into a form of life that is aware of itself: a human being.

What an enormous responsibility is placed on human beings! Given this awareness and the ensuing ability to doubt and question life, we are somehow torn apart from life: we not only live, but we also examine life as a phenomenon. How will we survive? How can we learn to live and, at the same time, be aware of this life as outsiders? These are tough questions.

So we embark on this journey called life to find answers. However, it is a finite journey. From the very beginning, this precious project of life has been programmed to self-destruct. But soon we begin to suspect that even this journey is not our final destination—somewhere far ahead lies a new mystery. Can anything make sense after this realization? How can we trust anything?

When we look at life as a series of wrenching changes, with death as the given conclusion, the thought of controlling life appears ridiculous. We truly have no choice but to take life as it comes, to open ourselves—willingly or unwillingly—to life's often messy embrace, the squeeze of birth that almost killed us and eventually will.

love carries us to safety

In this unrelenting embrace of life, one question rises above all others: How can we be safe? Where can we find safety when life entails such chaos and insecurity? Does this perpetual journey, this process of change and relinquishment, offer anything lasting and unaltered? Will anything ever provide such certainty that we will have the courage to trust the process of living?

These questions press inside every one of us, because we all know what will happen in the end. Whether figuratively or even literally, the ground will suddenly open and swallow us, drawing us into an abyss with no return. This awareness is imprinted on each of us—even those who have always avoided such thoughts.

The question of safety is in fact a question of love. Love reminds us that we are not alone and need not carry ourselves alone; rather, we are carried—we are supported throughout our journey. *Love car-*

ries us in all that we do. Love saves each of us from being the only security in our own lives and places our existence in a greater context. This context not only offers us true safety, but it also gives life its deepest meaning. Though we may not fathom the mysteries of life, might there be a power that does? Is there a being who knows where we come from and where we are going? If so, this being must know the answer to our most compelling questions: What is the meaning of life? Why must we die?

When the chasm opens under our feet at the end of our lives, we must be able to trust that someone will catch us, someone with arms strong enough to carry us in both life and death. Only then can we muster the courage to live fully, taking life as it unfolds. Without the awareness of being carried, we try to carry ourselves. We build a sense of security by shielding ourselves from life, hindering our journey.

we cling to self-made safety structures

The ways in which we try to build security on our own are manifold and inventive. Clinging to material things is one of the most common; we can assign so much meaning to material possessions that we eventually see them as *the* source of a safe and meaningful life. When we focus our mind and soul on amassing possessions, we soon become convinced that life is about material things. This conviction helps us keep the disturbing questions about life at bay.

Another strategy for feeling safe is to hold Western science in supreme regard, thereby creating the illusion that we in fact comprehend life. We can study thousands of books, subscribe to numerous papers, follow dozens of newscasts, and pursue multiple degrees, anticipating the answers of hard science to questions about life and death. Science believers employ knowledge to create artificial safety: by reducing reality to regularities and predictabilities, we reason, we can control it.

Clinging to others is not an uncommon security strategy. We can cling to our spouse, for example, like a child to a parent, and avoid the responsibilities of an adult, which include facing and acknowledging the fearsome unpredictability inherent in life. We can remain children and delegate our lives to someone else.

Many people cling to a religion, following a strict dogma of beliefs, norms, and regulations. When we reduce life to black and white, we feel certain precisely what is right and what is wrong; then we can side with the good against the bad—that is, against all the rest of humankind. This type of sectarianism is one of the most devious forms of evil, because the evil is masked by an image of utmost goodness. When we become this rigidly religious, we appoint ourselves in place of God, making God a servant of our own purposes. This is what Jesus considered his greatest enemy—and who eventually killed him? The good and the blameless.

We can also try to control reality with chronic niceness, by presenting a flattened and harmless version of ourselves in exchange for acceptance. Another word for this is *manipulation*: we deny others the opportunity of giving us an honest reaction; instead, we manipulate them into responding to us in a specific way. Using this approach, we never risk being vulnerable, and thus we deny ourselves the opportunity to be loved, for when we hide our human imperfections—our occasional crankiness and other fatal flaws—from others, we also hide them from love. Many people think that Christianity is about being nice: always turn the other cheek, even though your hand is clenched in a fist in your pocket. But when we examine Jesus's life, we see that he was far from nice and compliant. On the contrary, he was difficult—so much so that the established regime determined it essential to eliminate him as swiftly as possible.

Avoiding risks is a popular strategy for feeling safe: we refuse to try anything new in an effort to avoid making a mistake and having to face our human incompleteness. Instead, we always do the same things in the same way, trying to attain control by making our life uniform and predictable. We stay in the same job for thirty years, always eat the same foods, never meet new and different people, always spend our summer vacation in the same way, always dress in the same style—and always disdain those who are different and do things differently. This is the formula for *self-conceit*: we are convinced that we have reached our destination; others who are still on their journeys need our advice because we know how things should be. And we offer advice because we cannot afford to listen; after all, we might hear something new and shocking, something we would not be able to control. We also keep a distance because others might see in us something that we refuse to see, and the narrower our life, the more compelling our need to condemn and criticize others. We never see and hear others as who they really are; instead, we involve them in our inner drama and see them merely as a means of becoming more and more convinced that our way of life is superior.

We may also seek control by postponing life to some future time. Life will begin after we complete the doctoral dissertation, after we have children, after our children have grown up, after we pay off the mortgage, after we can afford a summer house, after the promotion we're waiting for, after retirement ... *then* we will have time for what we consider important: children, friends, spouse, health, spirituality, ourselves. I once heard a horrendous example of postponing life indefinitely: A couple consulting a lawyer wanted a divorce because their life together had been hell and they had never enjoyed each other's company. Both were over ninety years old! When the lawyer asked why they had not divorced earlier, the couple replied that they had been waiting for their children to die.

When we step out of the present moment, we step out of the only moment in which life is present. When we defer life to a later time, we never become involved. We can fill up our time with so many tasks that we never need to stop and face reality. When we have no time for reflection, we never need to face our emptiness and incompleteness. The greater our anguish, the faster our pace. The faster our pace, the greater our anguish. Ironically, we seem to flee from what we are chasing after: the experience of being loved and valued. We frantically search everywhere for something that we could find within, in our authentic being, our weakness, our humanity. If we could allow ourselves to communicate our weakness and helplessness, we would reach love and the conviction that we are good enough and entitled to a good life. We could attain what we are chasing after simply by stopping and being open to receiving it.

Other ways of hiding our human weakness include attempting to become perfect. When we decide that we know everything and know how to do everything right, we enter a territory where weakness is prohibited. We escape weakness by trying to achieve its opposite, perfection. When we are perfect, no one will ever be able to catch us in a mistake—but no one will ever be able to love us, either. The shield of perfection protects us from love, and in shielding against love we deny ourselves the opportunity for a genuine life.

We can also control life by becoming invisible, by making certain that we have no difficult opinions, needs, or feelings—better yet, no opinions at all. We hide our talents instead of using them, because being creative would attract attention, which is dangerous. When we efface ourselves so that we cannot be seen, we cease to be vulnerable. We no longer need anything from others, not even love; we no longer test our environment in any way or take up our rightful space. We do not take a stand, causing no trouble or inconvenience—and by never taking the risk of being seen for who we really are, we are in fact controlling our environment. We create safety by dismissing everything that hints at life. The price we pay for this may be high, but we feel no price is too high when safety is a critical priority.

Another safety structure is to live the life of others so that we need not live our own. We can focus on their affairs; we can consider, experience, and perceive matters from their viewpoint. In so doing, we avoid examining ourselves. The compulsive need to take care of others is a manifestation of this unhealthy self-sufficiency: we continually save others from the consequences of their actions; we help, understand, support, comfort, and encourage, even though no one asked us to. In focusing on others, we lose touch with ourselves almost completely.

Perhaps the most familiar example of a self-made safety structure is the wife of an alcoholic. She lets her life pass her by because of his drinking. The worse she feels in the relationship, the more she concentrates on trying to control his habit. The more responsibility she is willing to assume, the more he is free to drink. Thus she actually partakes in his alcoholism by saving him from the consequences of his drinking.

In our Western culture, substance abuse is probably the most common means of trying to control our life. Although it may seem that the abuser is seeking a release from self-control, the truth is just the opposite: we abuse substances to chemically manipulate our feelings. Instead of seeking the company of others and risking vulnerability by revealing our weakness and powerlessness, we turn to alcohol and other substances for solace and understanding. We exchange the genuine pleasure of closeness and connection for an artificially induced pleasure that, with the help of substances, we can produce ourselves. This is another attempt at shielding ourselves against love and retaining the illusion of total control over life.

Paradoxically, substance use often leads to addiction, the opposite of control—but the addict does not see this. Instead of acknowledging an addiction and asking for help, the addict strives for greater control over his habit. It makes sense, then, that the absence of a healthy sense of sickness is an essential characteristic of addiction. In addition to unhealthy self-sufficiency, this leads to deeper isolation, a new reason to medicate our feelings with substances. The spiral of addiction can be interrupted only by admitting our loss of control and asking for help. This is how life invites us back to communion—communion with others and with life itself.

we treat ourselves the way we were treated as children

A lack of love causes us to avoid approaching others. We do not wish to—or we dare not—reveal our powerlessness and human neediness; instead, we rely on ourselves and the more or less wobbly safety structures of our own making.

But where does this lack of love originate? Somewhere in the course of our journey, our experiences created the need to protect ourselves from others and from life, and as we isolate ourselves we become convinced that there is no love for us. These experiences may stem from different periods in our life; however, those from early childhood are engraved most deeply in our beings.

The way we were treated in our early years conveys an essential message about our value; in adulthood, we tend to treat ourselves accordingly. Those close to us define our worth by showing us or not showing us love. If we have plenty of experiences of being loved, we believe that we are lovable and treat ourselves with the same respect: we take good care of ourselves, consider our feelings and needs important, and do not allow ourselves to be treated otherwise.

On the other hand, if our experiences of being loved are few, we expect to be treated in an unloving way. Convinced of our unworthiness, we surround ourselves with people who treat us poorly—after all, we have learned to consider this normal. We may, for example, choose a spouse who is violent, alcoholic, disparaging, or otherwise negligent.

Through their behavior, others have told us who we are. This is especially true of those who were close to us in our tender stages of early development: our parents—biological or otherwise—who were entrusted with the responsibility for our budding lives.

lack of love in childhood is self-perpetuating

How is a lack of love manifested in childhood? Emotionally, parents who have not grown up are so engrossed in their own unfulfilled childhood needs that they have no place in their heart for a new child. This may even lead to reversed roles, and the child is expected to nurture the needy and wounded child that the parent carries within. And so this newcomer grows up without the presence of an adult: no one sees or hears what happens inside the young boy or girl. Children who have no experience of being seen or heard for who they really are grow into adults bereft of an authentic self, adults out of touch with their own depths.

Furthermore, the absence of a true adult's presence in childhood usually means that no one sets boundaries and defines clear roles in the family. As a result, children wield a power that should not belong to them—a power for which they are not emotionally and developmentally prepared. A child with this power inevitably feels insecure and holds contempt for the adults in the family, intuitively recognizing that the adults have failed to assume their rightful responsibility. A child who despises adulthood develops first into an adolescent who refuses to grow up, and later into a parent who does not care enough to raise his or her children, while endlessly seeking self-fulfillment—the fulfillment of neglected childhood needs.

Lack of love in childhood often manifests itself as shame—belittlement, disparagement, ridicule, scorn. The opposite of love, shame is quick to fill the void that a lack of love creates. Worse, shame crushes what love fosters—the emerging personality—in every way possible. Love shelters a vulnerable young personality.

In love, a parent may condemn a child's wrong *act*, but never his personality. We cannot connect with our authentic self without acknowledging and embracing our vulnerability, and we cannot reveal our vulnerability without the presence of love.

Someone setting conditions for us may also reflect a lack of love in our lives: *I will love you if you* . . . Love is not something to be earned. No one can control love by striving to become worthy. There may be a lack of love in families where everything appears to be perfect: families that have a good social standing, that are wealthy, educated, well traveled, and so on. But there is a problem when everything must *look* good: the impression we make becomes more important to us than the reality behind it, which is an inner emptiness. Lovelessness of this kind is often skillfully disguised and therefore hard to recognize: because everything *looks* so good, it seems that everything must *be* good.

Our experiences of lovelessness are woven into our personalities and, in adulthood, find expression in a lack of love for ourselves and our environment. This lack prevents us from trusting and approaching others: we never reveal our true selves. Instead, convinced that revealing our vulnerability would be dangerous, we hide from others and guard ourselves from being hurt by the loveless encounters we have come to expect.

inner safety leads to a life of courage

A lack of love always creates fear, for fear originates when we are left alone, without a deep connection to others—without love. Such fear leads to a need to control life rather than live it. And because we are unable to trust love, we dare not be weak. When we are overcome with fear, we also dare not make mistakes—they would reveal our human weakness. Thus, inner insecurity kills creativity.

It is love that provides safety, through a serene tolerance of the insecurity inherent in life; when love is present, we have the courage to truly live, even though living in itself *is* dangerous. We dare to try new things—including those we cannot control—free from the need to compensate for a lack of inner safety through a constant effort to ensure our outer safety. In other words, inner safety leads to an ability to live dangerously. And this introduces our third paradox: *If you seek safety, you must live dangerously.*

A dangerous life is a creative life, one that includes taking risks; the price we pay for this is always vulnerability. We cannot create anything new if we invariably depend on the old just because we are afraid of change. Therefore, a survival strategy based on an excessive need for safety actually kills life.

So what do we need in order to revive and gain the courage to continue our journey? How can a person trapped behind safety structures break free and resume the journey, this dangerous journey called life?

the sounds of life strengthen along the path of fear

Arising from a lack of love, fear is the reason behind unhealthy self-sufficiency and all the safety structures that we devise. When feeling fearful, we try to control life instead of living it; therefore, the path to a healthy life requires facing our fear. So if we feel that life is meaningless and empty, and nothing compelling ever happens to us, we need to start living dangerously.

What, then, is a dangerous life? Living dangerously means becoming who we are in our innermost being; that is to say, it means wrecking our elaborate security constructions and making contact with our authentic self. A dangerous life is about becoming visible, allowing our true personality to come forward.

This may not sound that dramatic or dangerous, but it is, very much so: we cannot approach our innermost being without abandoning the safety structures we have created. If we have built our feeling of security on alcohol, we have to give up this safety. If we have sought safety by clinging to knowledge and erudition, we have to become innocent and helpless, facing the fact that knowledge no longer guides our journey. If we are suffocating with riches, we must stop making money our main focus. If we cling to our spouse, delegating the responsibility for our life, we have to set our spouse free and learn how to stand on our own feet. If we cling to religion and black-and-white thinking, we have to muster the courage to step into freedom. If we have sought security by becoming harmless and invisible, we have to become visible again. If we have become chronically nice, we have to learn how to express our anger.

As we can see from these examples, change feels extremely dangerous. We have crafted our safety structures to protect ourselves from the feelings of great insecurity we have experienced at some stage—usually at an early age. When we begin to question and dismantle these structures, which seem to have provided our only safety, we must face those catastrophic feelings that caused us to erect them in the first place. So in the throes of change we may feel that our world is collapsing and we are losing our way and our sanity.

This is why many people do not venture to leave a destructive marriage. They dare not face the feelings of insecurity that being alone would bring to the surface; in fact, many people would rather die than face these fears. This also is one reason why many alcoholics cannot give up drinking; abandoning their only island of safety would uncover the feelings and issues behind the drinking. True recovery requires addressing these issues—although sobriety is a prerequisite, that alone is not enough.

Relinquishing our safety structures often evokes a fear so enormous that we are not willing to face this fear until we have no choice but to let go. Still, many people choose self-destruction over self-discovery.

courage is fear turned into prayer

Change often feels life-threatening, but there are those who are willing to take this course—this mission that may seem impossible. They all have something in common, a quality without which none of them would survive: courage.

Courage is perhaps the most admired of human attributes, yet it is difficult to define. Perhaps we do not have to define it, because we all know what courage is—or do we? We often think that to have courage means to be unafraid, but the opposite seems to be true: *courage is the ability to take action despite our fear*. Courage is a quality we need because of fear, that is to say, as a companion or counterforce to fear. We could even say that courage is a positive result of fear; the negative result would be allowing ourselves to be paralyzed.

Courage is fear turned into prayer, as someone aptly put it. I am taken with the unadorned truthfulness of these words. When faced with a seemingly insuperable task or situation, a courageous person realizes the limits of her resources; however, she cannot avoid or escape the overpowering situation. The supremacy of that which she must face forces her to her knees, and although the task seems impossible, something within her senses that it is not. As she tackles the impossible, she falls back on another seeming impossibility: God. Because the task at hand exceeds the limits of her abilities, she must resort to something beyond these limits, and here we have the origin of prayer. *Prayer is a courageous stand in the face of an overpowering task.* The courageous person prays *because* she is afraid. Hence, courage is a quality of being humble and understanding the limits of our resources.

a hero has faith in uncharted terrain

Courage is an essential quality of a hero—or, more accurately, courage makes a hero: a person who has the ability to listen to her innermost being and act accordingly. For this reason, however, she may come into conflict with the surrounding world, so a hero must also have the courage to stand alone. In facing her fear, a hero creates a new path for herself. She doesn't ask what she should create; instead, she listens to her innermost heart—her human core—and bravely takes a stand against existing institutions, structures, and conventions. Thus, the hero causes conflict and meets opposition: saboteurs inevitably follow her as she travels her lonely course. The true followers come later; sometimes the hero must even die before the path she created becomes the road to travel. Many artists spring to mind: Vincent van Gogh, for example, who lived poor and tormented and whose paintings nobody understood while he lived; today only the fabulously wealthy can afford one. Heroes have been burned at the stake, nailed to the cross, publicly mocked and ridiculed, banished from their homelands, held in contempt, rejected, derogated, and denounced as heretics.

As I have mentioned, heroes have a wondrous ability to believe in their innermost feelings more than in institutional practices. In their opposition to conventions, heroes threaten the illusion of control and the false sense of security that we have created. We humans have a tendency to force life into patterns, to systematize and subdue what once was vividly alive. Love, for example—something that should sweep us off our feet—develops into marriage, which at its most beautiful is sacred, but at its worst is a legal arrangement devoid of love. (As a popular joke puts it, a courtship can end in two ways: happily or in a marriage.)

In the same manner, *faith—a feeling of burning with enthusiasm, great passion, and a desire for reform*—develops into religion, a set of rules for earning salvation. Faith becomes religion when God is replaced with a more convenient and controllable system of beliefs. In other words, when we are not willing to live before God, we create a religion that tames faith and God into something within our control. Similarly, social justice attained through conflict and struggle becomes legislation, an invention becomes a patent, a social movement becomes a political party, a revolution becomes a political system, a creation becomes fashion, a delicate insight becomes a trend.

When a movement or issue develops into an institution, it loses contact with its original purpose, and the motivating passion and glow inevitably wane. An institution has a life of its own. Bureaucracy is a fine example of this: bureaucracy is said to maintain itself, becoming its own purpose; instead of serving people, it expects to be served. A public servant is a servant no more.

A hero recognizes these lifeless systems that offer security but kill spontaneity. Heroism means defying these dead institutions that nurture unquestioned conformity, that offer acceptance only to those who cling to set patterns, always doing everything in the same manner as everyone else. And so, when a hero shakes off these shackles, those who cling to the systems begin to feel uncertain. Their safety threatened, they react vehemently—they may even be willing to kill the hero to protect the illusion of safety that the empty fortress provides.

our inner prince meets our inner dragon

We know from history of many great men and women who changed the course of humankind by believing in things that were not yet known but eventually came into existence because these heroes stubbornly stood by their convictions. We all know who Martin Luther King Jr., Gandhi, Columbus, Galileo Galilei, and Johann Sebastian Bach were. We also know who Jesus of Nazareth was.

But do we know who John Smith and Jane Doe are? They are heroes, too, even though their names are not mentioned when history is written. And why are they heroes? Because in the end heroism is about having the courage to grow up: becoming an adult means defying the inner images from our childhood.

When we were little, we faced the crushing superiority of adults. They were, to begin with, physically so mighty that we were powerless over them; their knowledge and skills were also vastly superior to ours. We internalized these images of our superior parents, and these developed into inner institutions, so to speak. These institutions offered us safety as long as we obeyed, as long as we did as our parents wished or told us to do. When we were children, our lives were completely dependent on our parents, and this feeling continues with our internalized parents: we still feel that our survival depends on doing their will.

Sometimes these internalized parents represent forces that repress our independence. We must somehow find the courage to defy and fight these internalized rules that conflict with our individuality—demolishing our source of safety in life. This struggle to break free from internalized conventionalities is described in many fairy tales in which the prince must fight a dragon, which represents his horrifically mighty parents; the prince stands for freedom, individuality, independence, and adulthood. In the dragon, the prince faces crushing superiority, with the dragon wielding the same power his parents held over him as a child.

The prince is an archetypal image of a hero: when the prince defeats the dragon, individuality overcomes inner conventionality. Here we see that heroism is in fact an everyday matter; each day is a battlefield where our inner prince meets our inner dragon. But what could this everyday heroism mean in practice?

heroes have the courage to approach their authentic self

A hero is, for example, a person who has the courage to leave a lifeless marriage. The hero has the courage to do so in spite of conventional disapproval: some people will undoubtedly regard her as irresponsible or even sinful. However, she believes more strongly in her innermost feelings, which tell her that lovelessness is a sin, as is maintaining an arrangement merely for the sake of appearances, fearful of growth and change. Many well-meaning Christians oppose divorce—not because divorce is a sin, but because confronting the possibility of divorce in their lives would require encountering their own fears. They hide behind grand words, such as God and morals, so that they need not meet their fears; they cloak themselves in righteousness to be safe, at least temporarily, from their own inner need or pressure to change. They seem to be motivated by good intentions, but their true motivation is fear.

This is nothing new. The Pharisees tried to intimidate Jesus with their religion and their descent as the heirs to Abraham. But Jesus refused to be intimidated, for, as John the Baptist put it, God can raise up children for Abraham from stones. When faith becomes an institution, it turns into religiousness, which rarely has room for God. Furthermore, rigid religiousness is seldom a practical tool for life. Many Christians who condemn divorce are actually trapped in their own loveless marriages, which they, for fear of being judged as failures and sinners, dare not leave. But God is love: He wants love in our lives, not a hollow institution that is merely called love.

A hero may have the courage not to divorce, even though everyone else seems to think he should. If he truly believes that the hurt in the marriage can be worked through and healed, he is a hero for staying and heeding his inner conviction. If he feels this is the right and the loving thing to do, he should do it, even though "well-meaning" people may despise him for it. The greatest evil in the world is malice disguised as goodness, but our hero ignores it.

A hero has the courage to resign from a workplace where she does not feel comfortable and where changes for the better seem unlikely. Before reaching this decision, however, she will have offered her work community an opportunity to address the issues that are causing discord. She does not flee from the problems in the workplace. But if no change takes place, she is not willing to sacrifice herself or her health—she leaves, even though people may think she is crazy to leave the security of a regular income. She takes the risk, living dangerously and creatively, looking forward to what will happen when she takes her personal value seriously and is true to herself rather than silently conforming.

A hero also has the courage to risk rejection by expressing anger in situations in which he has always been nice and compliant. He understands that peace at any cost is not necessarily the best solution; sometimes we must break peace by creating a crisis, if harmony has been maintained only by avoiding difficult issues. Such a peace is always a worse option than a crisis created by bringing forth the truth—by facing problems as they really are. Expressing anger ends the artificial niceness that smothers any opportunity to change and grow. Tolerating all wrongs and structural faults in an organization does not constitute loyalty; on the contrary, true loyalty to the workplace means addressing all the difficulties the community needs to work through so as to grow and develop. A hero has the courage to stir up a stagnant situation.

Heroism is also about revealing our vulnerability. When we expose our vulnerability, we become more honest: when someone hurts us, we have the courage to show that we are hurt. A seemingly strong person may act as though nothing has happened; then her concealed hurt feelings become a barrier to closeness. When she again meets the person whose actions hurt her, her smile is no longer natural—something has come between the two of them.

Emotional honesty means that we take our feelings seriously and communicate them to others: this creates true closeness. Of course, emotional honesty can also bring us pain, for there are always people who will take advantage of this vulnerability and step on us so as to appear a little taller. Then again, a hero is not only courageous, but also sensible and free to use her judgment to recognize those who prey on vulnerability.

Heroism may also mean talking when previously we have kept silent—or it may mean being silent when we were once eager to open our mouths. We may decide to voice our opinion about something that needs to be addressed but that others are trying their best to avoid, or we may choose to simply listen and trust that we are acknowledged, even though we are not actively asserting ourselves. Silence is often wiser than words; again, the hero is free to use her judgment.

Heroism may mean having faith when we once were cynical. Faith, openly expressed, makes us vulnerable; cynicism is a way of hiding our vulnerability. The cynical person hopes to be seen as an intellectual, a sophisticate; he has a horror of appearing childish or naive. In intellectual circles, being childish—that is, like a child in openness and trust—takes immense courage; however, the greatest truths of life are revealed only to the childlike—the complacent cynics must settle for fabrications of their own making.

It also takes courage to choose not to believe purported truths and dogmas proclaimed by an authority. Religious sects are adept at manipulating reality when the pure truth presents a threat that they feel must be eliminated. A hero has the courage to face truths that puncture the inflated self-importance of our religious authorities. As we can see from these examples, both childlike faith and sensible thinking can require courage, depending on what type of blind believers surround us.

Silence Is Golden

Lately I have found myself fascinated by a specific form of heroism: the kind that refuses to rush. We live in a society in which chronic hurrying prevails. Lack of time has become an indication of importance and a way of amassing self-esteem. If you are not in a constant hurry, you are a nobody. If your calendar or personal organizer or time management system is not full, you are nothing. If your cell phone does not ring constantly, you have reason to doubt your existence. If you are not busy, you are useless.

I am currently in the middle of great changes, in the process of instigating a four-year training program for those in the helping professions on how to meet their clients as *people* rather than as patients or other administrative entities. Many things demand my attention: phone calls, e-mails, letters, interviews . . . At the same time, I am supposed to be writing a book—but creative work requires an unhurried state of mind: silence, space, room for thought. Such tranquility, however, is elusive if you allow daily matters to control you instead of controlling them. But do I have the courage to make space for creative thinking? Do I have the courage to say no? Do I have the courage to enter a silence in which my cell phone does not ring, my calendar has appropriate blank space, and no one assures me how important and essential I am? Being unavailable takes great courage, because in so doing you say no to potentially interesting projects—if you commit to one above all, you cannot commit to hundreds of others.

This tranquil state of mind does not simply happen; we must choose to create the silence and space. But challenging the prevailing way of life takes courage. Many people dream about quitting the rat race; they talk and talk and talk about it with great longing, but few actually quit. Why? Because in abandoning that which is considered normal we enter a great loneliness, a pathless terrain—and this is always frightening. When we enter this terrain, we can see tracks of a dragon, and we know that, sooner or later, we must face this beast.

The Hero's Path Is Lonely

A hero abandons the safety of seeing the emperor's new clothes. When she points out that the emperor is naked, she detaches herself from her community and loses the safety and support it has given her. She enters the painful loneliness that arises when we oppose rules and institutions. Perhaps the hero is actually a creation of the community, a creation needed for renewal. Could it be that—after an institution's original purpose has died and it has begun to smother life—the collective subconscious creates a demand for a hero who is willing to enter this great, archetypal loneliness? There is no heroism without loneliness. This loneliness signals that something genuinely new is being created, something outside the dead conventionalities that prevail.

Jesus faced this archetypal loneliness on the cross: "My God, my God, why have you forsaken me?" This experience of loneliness is our surest sign that he truly created something new. His cry from the cross was the cry of creation. It said that someone in humanity had stepped out of everything safe and known in this world, creating a connection between earth and heaven—and an opportunity for us to be born again, from above. To truly grow, we must be willing to face this archetypal loneliness, and the cry of creation must be heard from our mouths. Without heroism, there is no growth; without growth, there is no life.

a disaster is not always a disaster

If we wish to regain our authentic life, we must be willing to face heroic loneliness. This triggers feelings of immense insecurity, which is why we often cling to the safety that conventionality offers: we do as others do and bow low before those institutions that reward our loyalty. But what happens when these institutions begin to smother us? What happens when safety turns into a prison in which we lose our sense of being alive? What happens when the current of life ceases to flow around us and the standing water begins to stink?

When we have worked through catastrophes in life, we usually appreciate different things than we did before, and our values deepen. This may happen, for example, when a loved one dies or when a baby is born—life is so powerfully present in both birth and death that we would have to be totally numbed not to notice.

A catastrophe can also come in the form of unemployment, illness, accident, alcoholism, or divorce. These all are crises that may shake our life so profoundly that they actually present us with an opportunity to begin anew. These experiences feel cruel and pointless at first, but we may be thankful afterward. Why? Because these catastrophes shatter the safety that we have built precisely to avoid the insecurity inherent in life.

It is not uncommon for people to pray spontaneously when they face a crisis. A prayer is a cry for someone to help carry us when we have lost the strength to carry ourselves; in other words, seeking and faith seem to originate when we are broken. Our lives and values become deeper when we come close to reaching our limits. I think it is fair to say that catastrophes may even bring us back to life.

Instead of waiting until a great catastrophe strikes, we can learn how to create smaller ones to keep us alive; we can learn how to make choices that keep us from falling into hibernation, a somnolent state of false security. What does this mean? Essentially the same thing as being heroic: when we dismantle whatever has offered us safety, we create an insecurity that makes us seek a source of deeper safety, true and lasting safety. If we hang on for dear life to the safety structures we have erected, we will never find out whether such true safety exists. If we never do anything that scares us, if we always choose that which feels safe and familiar, never confronting our limits—we will never grow.

Heroism involves seeking situations that evoke fear, that allow us to get in touch with our fears. We are afraid of what we cannot control, so our fears indicate the direction we should choose in our effort to grow. When we begin to try things that scare us, we lose control. If our fears have suffocated our life, this is the best thing that could happen to us.

But what are we so afraid of?

our dreams tell us who we will be in the future

Our fears are mysteriously connected to the future we envision. And our dreams are part of the authentic personality waiting to be born within us, yet unknown—of which we are afraid. We have trouble identifying with our true self because we have never had the chance to explore our authentic being. Many of us grew up in an environment in which only a small part of us was acknowledged, so only a small part of our authentic self came into existence; however, our unborn and unknown qualities are still part of us. Our dreams are signals of this unknown within us.

A hero sincerely listens to her dreams and has the courage to follow them. She bases her choices on her dreams and commits herself to her inner visions so strongly that they begin to come true. In so doing, she comes into conflict with both the conventionality in her community and the conventionality within: though something in her believes in her vision, something does not. This is when she must become a hero and fight her inner dragon, remaining true to her dreams.

A hero comes into conflict with those who have decided not to listen to their dreams but instead have chosen false safety. When the hero, although warned not to, nevertheless heads out to fight the dragon, she reminds those who are clinging to safety of their choice, their decision to stay stagnated and not to fight.

to have faith is to have courage

Faith originates in everyday heroism: if we are willing to demolish our safety structures by making brave choices, we face a terrifying insecurity. As previously noted, courage is fear turned into prayer. When living dangerously and creatively, a hero must have faith in something greater than himself.

We lack faith and spirituality in our culture not so much because faith is valued less than intellect (with the view that to be a believer you must be a wide-eyed fool), but because it is hard for us to believe that if we run out of strength we somehow will still be carried.

In fact, faith is difficult because we have a hard time believing that we are loved. The question of God is fundamentally a question of love: if we do not believe that we are carried by a loving God, we will never have the courage to truly live. We will try to control life instead of simply living it. But we can find safety only by facing our insecurity.

CHAPTER 4

what you give up will be given to you

In our culture, ownership and material things have become a means to constructing an identity. Materialism is the religion of our time; we turn to it for meaning and significance, as though we have lost contact with our human core and so lost our chance to live a deep life. This creates a void that we then try to cover with material abundance: the more material goods, we seem to think, the better our lives will be.

But as we all know, superficial abundance cannot compensate for the lack of a deep life. In fact, the opposite seems to be true: the more material wealth we collect to conceal our emotional malaise, the worse we seem to feel.

Inner distress cannot be cured with external measures, no matter how we try to adorn ourselves. What is the connection between our inner and outer well-being—or is there a connection? For example, if outer success does not necessarily lead to inner success, what does? And does outer success automatically follow inner success; in other words, when we feel better emotionally, are we also more likely to attain material success? This raises a more provocative question: can a rich person feel well emotionally, or does material wealth necessarily entail emotional distress? This question may seem humorous or even absurd—depending on the amount of amassed wealth in question—but it is justified since our entire culture is founded on an appreciation of material wealth. So *is* it possible for us to be wealthy and, at the same time, feel well emotionally? If yes, then what type of person has the emotional resources to cope with material wealth?

"but seek first His kingdom and His righteousness, and all these things will be given to you as well"

The New Testament offers an interesting response to our questions, so let us consider the pertinent passage in more detail. After all, the existence of this passage suggests that these questions were already relevant long before Western civilization made a religion of acquisition.

"All These Things Will Be Given"?

According to my understanding, "all these things" refers to earthly possessions—which we Western people have made the main content of our existence and which we believe to be the source of a good life. This material good "will be given" to us; in other words, according to Jesus, we cannot achieve wealth by striving for it. Jesus turns our hierarchy of values upside down, making material good a secondary matter for which we should not struggle. Instead, it "will be given" to us when our values fall into the right order; that is to say, when we "seek first his kingdom."

But what is this mysterious kingdom? For us to seek this kingdom, as Jesus advises, we should probably have some sort of idea of what it is; after all, seeking always aims at finding, and we cannot seek something of which we have no notion. Jesus often spoke of "his kingdom" or the "heavenly kingdom." This wording led many of his contemporaries astray: they began awaiting something visible, hopeful of a messianic revolution that would free Israel from Rome.

Even today, the meaning is still unclear. His words evoke the kind of distant fairy-tale kingdom we yearned for as children, a Sunday-school world of gilded streets and ethereally beautiful angels. Many people think that seeking the heavenly kingdom must mean becoming religious, adopting religious habits and rituals; however, Jesus dismissed religiousness of this type, saying, for example, that the Sabbath was made for man, not man for the Sabbath. He meant that religious rules and habits should not become so important that we become slaves to them.

Clearly, the concept of a heavenly kingdom can be twisted by turning it into a manifestation of starry-eyed fantasy or manmade religiousness, a form of unhealthy self-sufficiency. But could the mysterious kingdom he spoke of mean something much more? Could it be something that has significance in our everyday lives? Could understanding this concept, even a little bit, bring relief to our emotional discontent? In truth, the entire message of Christianity seems to be intended for the everyday, our lives in the here and now; divine fairy-tale worlds have little to offer us when we seek help in our distress. But how can we unravel the true and practical meaning of the heavenly kingdom? This kingdom seems impossible to define—but perhaps we can gather different aspects and see what image they create.

"His Kingdom"?

First, the heavenly kingdom appears to be something that is inside us: translated from Greek, the expression Jesus used means "within you" or "among you"—not in some fabled far-off sphere, but "closer to me than I am to myself," as Saint Augustine so beautifully put it. If the heavenly kingdom is among us, it must be where we live our everyday lives: this kingdom is in the midst of our interaction and communication; it is in what I say to you and what you say to me; it is what we are to each other and what we do to each other.

In other words, this heavenly kingdom is present in the way we greet the cashier at the supermarket. It is in the smile we give to the person next to us in the bus on a Monday morning. It may be present in the way we let a car in ahead of us in a traffic jam, or when we bake little buns for our family or set the table. It may even be present in the colorful new shirt we have decided to wear, even though we are afraid that the color will attract notice and make us too visible. Maybe the heavenly kingdom is also present in the way we set the newspaper aside and grin joyfully at the child who is playing at our feet.

Although present in all these concrete ways, the heavenly kingdom is, at the same time, something that does not submit to our control: it is always greater than our attempts to define and thus control it. We can interpret this kingdom and its effects psychologically, but we can never completely understand it; we can sense this kingdom and be touched by it, but we can never capture or control these encounters. The heavenly kingdom arouses our wonder and admiration, but it may also arouse our impatience and irritation, because it eludes our control. For this reason, we may oppose the heavenly kingdom and try to sabotage or deny it. We may even hate or despise this kingdom and seek to destroy it.

The heavenly kingdom, which represents truth, may also arouse fear or respect, revealing us as naked and vulnerable. We may be overcome and enthralled by this kingdom; it may light in us a fire that changes our lives. Or it can feel threatening, as it shocks, breaks barriers, and creates conflict.

Above all, the heavenly kingdom is about love: it brings us together and creates closeness. The heavenly kingdom is in fact the kingdom of love: if we live in faith, we live in love, for living in faith means believing that we are loved. And we cannot love others until we are convinced that we are loved. We enter the heavenly kingdom loved and live there lovingly, and faith is the vessel or vehicle that takes us there.

Faith also brings us hope. *Hope means awaiting good things in the future, believing that we will be loved in the future as well.* The essence of faith and hope is thus the same: being loved.

The heavenly kingdom is something for which we deeply long, because something deep in our being does not find a home on this earth. It is as though something within us was not meant for this world—a void within that only the heavenly kingdom can fill. The presence of the heavenly kingdom thus arouses powerful feelings of homecoming: there we find our true identity. We were created as an image of God, and we can find this image deep within, where our authentic self lies. Our longing for the heavenly kingdom reflects the existence of this deeper identity; this is why the heavenly kingdom is also called *home* and *our heavenly home*—it gives us solace, meaning, and direction. Not even death controls our relationship with this kingdom, which spans the division between life and death as we know it, thus suggesting something greater than the life we now know.

All this is the heavenly kingdom that we should seek. But what does it mean to pursue this kingdom?

"But Seek First"?

For us to pursue something, it must arouse both our interest and our curiosity. Pursuing means concentrating our attention on something and seeking in that direction; seeking is about persistence, about not giving up, even though we may not make any immediate discoveries. Seeking is also about hope: we must be convinced that one day we will find what we are looking for. Otherwise our seeking would be in vain; should we learn for certain that the object of our seeking has ceased to exist, we would stop our quest.

Seeking has to do with waiting, waiting patiently, but it also is an active process that requires invention: we must constantly come up with new and creative ways of seeking in the right direction. Seeking often involves enthusiasm, an anticipation of the joy in finding our target. Enthusiasm is the driving force behind seeking, the energy that makes us continue despite setbacks. But the process of seeking also involves disappointment and hopelessness: we may decide to give up, to never again waste a thought on what we were seeking—until a newfound fervor arises and we return to our quest.

"Seek First His Kingdom"?

If we now combine the different aspects of seeking and of the heavenly kingdom, what will we see? We may come to the following conclusion:

Pursuing the heavenly kingdom is an unremitting zest for the unexplainable truth that we anticipate within.

This definition tells us that the heavenly kingdom is inside us. This kingdom is inexplicable; it can be anticipated, but not captured. At the same time, however, the heavenly kingdom is so powerful that we continue to pursue it despite frustration and disappointment. The heavenly kingdom also explains the nature of our existence; pursuing this kingdom means seeking the truth about the essence of our being. We could also describe seeking the heavenly kingdom as a dynamic process: it is more about moving *toward* a destination than about *reaching* one.

"But seek first his kingdom and his righteousness, and all these things will be given to you as well." What could this mean? Perhaps Jesus was saying something along these lines:

First seek what is within, what lights your soul ablaze; seek what arouses your wonder and what you cannot control. Seek love, create communion, be truthful, and reveal your vulnerability even though it may hurt; love hurts, but the hurt will heal you. Therefore be small, helpless, and lost, and when everything seems hopeless, trust that you will be carried. Never abandon hope; seek what you believe in your innermost being, even though it may seem impossible.

"Seek first his kingdom" could mean all of this.

"my kingdom come, my will be done!"

The greatest tragedy of humankind is that we do not know that we live in the heavenly kingdom; in other words, we do not believe that we are loved. We do not know that we are meant to live with an awareness of being carried. So we take life into our own hands and begin to build "our kingdom," and our prayer reads: "*My* kingdom come, *my* will be done on earth as it is in heaven." This means that we *seek* "all these things" instead of trusting that they *will be given* to us.

When we enter our own kingdom, we lose the opportunity for a deep life, and in turn we lose the chance for an authentic identity, because only in our depths can we find our true self and the life we were meant to live. If we wish to live a good life, we need to live a deep life—and to find this depth, we must turn inward. We cannot compensate for a lack of depth in our lives by focusing on the surface. In answer to our earlier questions, no, seeking and achieving outer success does not bring inner satisfaction. A successful life has more to do with inner than outer success. In fact, clinging to external success can be a sign of inner failure: the greater the need to amass symbols of success, the greater the failure. If we invest everything in what we have on the outside, we lose our inner life—and when we lose our inner life, we lose our self. Jesus asked, "What good will it be for a man if he gains the whole world, yet forfeits his soul?"

Losing our inner life means losing our peace of mind, and this always leads to loss of meaning: when we are not connected with our human core, we no longer know why we live. A person who has everything may feel that nothing is important. The life of the extremely rich is often a tragic struggle against loneliness and emptiness. Utter success in outer life may lead to absolute disaster in inner life—what better examples than the tragedies of Elvis Presley and Marilyn Monroe? Both were admired by the entire world, but both eventually destroyed themselves.

Our Inner Self May Go Unnoticed

When we lose our inner life, we do not always notice. Life feels empty, but we think this is just because we have not yet acquired enough. This is often true of people who are not aware of an inner life in the first place. Those of us who spent our childhood in a loveless home may be completely unaware of our inner depth, for we can find this dimension only in loving interaction with others. Having no contact with this depth, we feel that we are missing something, but we do not know what it is. Everything simply feels empty. To fill this emptiness, we resort to various means, all with one thing in common: unhealthy self-sufficiency, the pursuit of "my kingdom." The most common of these means include alcohol, work, money, impressive titles, knowledge, achievements, falling in love, food, bodybuilding, home decorating, sex, the Internet, power, religion, drugs, shopping, traveling, and entertainment—which all make tantalizing promises of a good life.

Now these things, in and of themselves, are not inherently bad; they are generally neutral or even good—when used wisely. Alcohol promises pleasure, relief, and good times. Money offers an opportunity to fulfill needs and realize dreams. Falling in love brings excitement and an intensity of feeling; religiousness adds depth and meaning to our existence. The Internet promises adventure, new contacts and opportunities, and a wider world. Achievements bring appreciation and contacts with exciting people. Food is absolutely necessary for nourishment and continued life; sex offers sensuality and a deep connection—and, needless to say, procreation and families.

Our Needs Make Us Vulnerable

We strive for things to enhance our well-being and the quality of our lives—fulfilling healthy, natural needs. Our needs are rich and reflect our humanity, but they make us vulnerable. Whenever we need something, we always need it *from someone*; without this connection, we cannot experience closeness or true appreciation. Our needs are the motive behind love, because they bring us into contact with others: to be seen and heard, we need someone who sees and hears us. In other words, our needs maintain love, a healthy dependency between people. Perhaps it is not incorrect to say that our human needs drive us to seek the heavenly kingdom, the kingdom of love.

Because our needs make us vulnerable, we often encounter disappointments; not all people are safe, not all can give us what we need. In addition to disappointment, we experience maltreatment, mockery, and even abandonment; if this happens early in childhood, we miss out on experiences of feeling good and secure when close to someone else. If we are wounded often enough, we begin to feel that others are dangerous and we had better hide our true needs and become strong and independent. And so our human needs remain unfulfilled. This in turn causes emotional illness, the true nature of which we fail to understand, so we seek to medicate our feelings with something that promises comfort and joy—alcohol, for example, or respect, or sex. We take the wrong medication: we seek not the "heavenly kingdom" but "all these things."

However, we should not *seek* "all these things" because "all these things" *will be given to us*. The earthly good should be a by-product, not a priority.

When our values become superficial and we take life into our own hands, we try to resolve our lives without leaning on others—without love. We pursue *our* kingdom, clinging obsessively to whatever we think is the deepest source of pleasure. When our values are in the right order, we "seek first his kingdom"—that is, we focus our attention on the unexplainable truth that we anticipate within.

when love withdraws, we take life into our own hands

We hear that our values have become superficial—but what does this mean? What are superficial values and what are deep ones? Love is the deepest value in this world; everything else should be based on this fact: we should "seek first" the kingdom of love. When this value falls into its rightful place, *everything* falls into place, and "all these things" that make heavenly promises of a good life—such as money, sex, and power—find their proper context, their true meaning and value.

But when our values are superficial, "all these things" become an end, not a means to an end. We pursue money for the sake of money, not as a means to a greater good. In so doing, we detach money from its original purpose, which is to serve others, and reduce it to a means of seeking selfish pleasure. Then money is no longer in the service of love.

The same happens with sex, which we have detached from erotic sensuality. Sex ceases to be a deeply sensual meeting of two people; instead, both parties use each other to fulfill their own needs, and both feel an emptiness: no profound closeness, no soulful interaction.

Interactions Are Abandoned

Impressions become important when our encounters with others lack genuine interaction and dialogue—that is, love. In these encounters, our intention is not to truly meet the other, but to make a favorable impression. No interaction is needed when we use others to improve our own value: the other person is not a subject, but an object.

Moreover, selfish enjoyment becomes more desirable than true interaction. When we use chemical substances to produce comforting pleasure, we try to fulfill our human needs without communion. Alcohol and drugs become a means to avoid closeness, and when we avoid genuine interaction, we escape from revealing our vulnerability—we may need others only as drinking buddies whose company alleviates the guilt we feel about our own drinking.

When love no longer guides our interactions with others, power goes astray. Originally intended as a means to serve others, power becomes a means in itself, an instrument that serves only our own objectives. Outside the context of love, we separate power from its original purpose: responsibility. Power acquired through responsibility and service is loving power. Without this responsibility, power is arbitrary, causing mischief, misconduct, injustice, or even violence.

Morals Become Elastic

When our values become superficial, our morals become elastic: nothing is absolute; everything depends on personal judgment and our chosen point of view. All is relative, and we may do as we wish, because nothing matters greatly in the end—as long as we feel good and have fun and get whatever we happen to want without much bother.

Religiousness becomes more important than faith. This means that we make ourselves the center of our religion: instead of praying for faith, we construct a system that we can control with our rules and demands. We do not trust that someone will have mercy on us, that someone will carry us when we do not have the strength; instead, we believe we can regulate life—and even regulate God.

When superficial values prevail, guilt becomes a mere feeling—a feeling, however, that disturbs the comfort of our lives. And no matter what, no one should feel guilty, right? Remorse does not feel good—so we try to abolish guilt. Life is no longer a mission; rather, life should always be fun, and God should be fun—a cosmic teddy bear that we can play with. Thus we no longer ask what life expects from us; we make demands. Shunning the natural drama inherent in life, we seek entertainment, which replaces life's true meaning and feeling of purpose.

Because setting limits is not pleasant, parents reject the role of being responsible for their children; instead, they try to become their children's best buddies. Parenting is no longer a special mission when morals are elastic; there is no need for them to pass on any particular ethics or standards to the next generation. Unfortunately, parents are so preoccupied with making certain that their children are busy and entertained that they do not realize they are preparing them for a lifetime of emptiness.

When our values become superficial, intoxication replaces sensual awareness. We no longer appreciate the natural beauty that the world offers; we want more! And because we feel empty, nothing ordinary—indeed, nothing short of fabulous—will do. To feel aroused and excited, we need to boost the pleasure chemically. As we lose sensitivity, we must pump up the volume to feel something, anything.

Haste Wastes Lives

When our values become superficial, we are always busy: we must seek more and more of everything, because we never receive what we truly need. This leads to constant hurry, which does not simply happen to us—we create unremitting haste with our poor choices.

We make those poor choices because we have lost touch with our innermost being; we amass all these things and then have no time for them. We are in a hurry because we want to be in a hurry. We complain that we do not have enough time for what we should do or would like to do, but our choices are always based on our own values. We do have time for what we consider truly important: if your hair is ablaze, you can certainly find time to put out the fire!

we flee from what we are chasing after

When we seek "all these things"—even things that can be good in and of themselves—they turn into monsters that take control and give us something other than what we were seeking, something completely different.

The alcoholic seeks joy, happiness, and the good life, but finds despair, shame, and degradation. He strives for the good, but finds his world shattered. The drug addict seeks fantastic experiences but finds a lethal addiction. The workaholic strives for respect and admiration but gets an ulcer, a stroke, or a divorce. The person seeking power gains not influence, but intrigue—a game in which the main purpose is to secure a great career by calculating each move with cunning. Someone seeking relief from feelings of guilt finds shame, which gains ground whenever guilt is not acknowledged. We can gain self-respect only by facing our guilt; shame does just the opposite, destroying our authentic self when it is most fragile. When we try to escape from our guilt, we flee from what we truly long for: dignity and integrity.

When we seek freedom by making absolute values relative, we lose our true freedom: the freedom to do what we know to be right. In so doing, we turn our wants into our values; over time, these values imprison us, and we feel compelled to always do what our desires prompt us to do—this is what happens in substance addiction.

The person who seeks sex finds pornography. When sex is detached from its original purpose—closeness and affection between two people and the potential for creating a new life—sex loses its soul and spirit.

What happens to cool parents who want to be pals with their children? They lose their children's respect, because children know instinctively that their parents should be responsible for setting safe limits. When parents seek to please their children by being permissive, instead of admiration they find contempt.

Someone who makes money the main purpose of her life soon finds herself in a cage—golden, admittedly, but still a cage. She is most likely alone in this cage, having created her vast fortune at the expense of others. She is surrounded not by friends but by people who pretend to be her friends in hopes of social and financial gains.

God owns everything we have

If we seek power, we must give up our pursuit and take responsibility instead. Taking responsibility means accepting a mission of service—no matter whether we are politicians or parents. We will gain power when we stop seeking power and begin to do what we know to be right in our innermost being. In this endeavor we will never run out of work, for correcting the injustice in this world requires an unlimited workforce. If we take this work seriously, before long we will become so important to our community that we gain influence. True power is influence: when we have gained influence through serving our community, we have a different attitude than do those who seek power just for the sake of power. We see power as a tool for our mission of service, not as an end in itself or a way to bolster our status. Thus we have no need to cling to power, and we are willing to abandon it; in fact, we seek to abandon power as soon as our mission allows for it. A politician is sincere if his main purpose is not to create a career but to gain influence to complete his mission for the common good—and to abandon power when he no longer needs it for this mission.

We can experience true sexuality only if we stop seeking sex. Sexuality is present in mutual respect, closeness, and affection between two people; these conditions are not possible without an emotionally secure and nurturing relationship. Emotional security is not possible without deep respect for each other—and impossible in a relationship in which we use the other to satisfy our selfish desires. When we feel emotionally secure, we have the courage to let our guard down, take the risk of closeness, reveal our vulnerability, and give something of ourself—only then can we experience true sexuality as a whole person. The sexual act becomes a caring and nurturing act, and we may reach such a level of soulful intimacy that it becomes a healing act: the nonverbal language of total, tender understanding can heal the lingering wounds from traumatic experiences.

We can free ourselves from feelings of guilt only by facing and acknowledging our guilt and in so doing gain self-respect. If we try to hide our guilt, the skeletons will continue to clatter in our closet; constantly aware of their presence, we must be on guard, because the skeletons might fall and tumble out the door. This awareness gradually begins to erode our identity: we have trouble respecting ourselves, knowing we have secrets to guard. We invest a great deal of energy in keeping that closet door shut, even though we would be free from all of this if we opened the door and faced our greatest fear, once and for all. We can free ourselves from guilt by freeing ourselves to *feel* the guilt—and move beyond it.

Inner Richness Is True Success

We can become rich by finding our inner richness. *True success is always inner success: outer life in harmony with inner life.* We then know who we are; we know our needs, dreams, and talents, and we listen to them. When we take our needs and dreams seriously, we can use our talents appropriately. In so doing, we create a life in which our most fundamental needs are fulfilled, and, because we live the life we most deeply want to live, we also serve others and our community in the best possible way. We find this inner richness when we stop pursuing outer wealth.

Money is a means, not a purpose. But what happens if the life we most deeply want to live also leads to material wealth? When money is not a goal, we do not cling to our material possessions; rather, we are emotionally prepared for the fact that we may lose our property at any time. We feel humble and thankful, because we know that we do not deserve any of our wealth. We do not make demands for material goods; the wealth we have is more a source of wonderment.

Can we create material wealth for ourselves by seeking a deep life? Does inner success always lead to material success? Can we seek "all these things" by pursuing the heavenly kingdom? No, because "all these things" are *given to us*. They are a gift—something we cannot earn, whether through service or struggle or otherwise.

Because a gift cannot be earned, receiving one requires humility: we should be able to simply accept the gift with gratitude. Seen in this light, only a humble person can cope with wealth; only a humble person can adopt an attitude toward it that does not lead to destruction. When we think that we are entitled to immense material wealth, we begin to defend our possessions. We want to make certain that we can keep our riches for ourselves, and we may want to amass more to prevent our property from shrinking over time. But when this becomes our focus, we are not seeking "first his kingdom" or even "all these things"—we are trying to *secure* "all these things." Jesus said that it would be hard for a rich person to enter the kingdom of heaven; however, he added that "with God all things are possible." Perhaps we could say that the right attitude toward the heavenly kingdom enables us to cope appropriately with earthly wealth: we may have everything, but own nothing. God owns everything we have. Thus the fourth paradox we encounter is: *What you give up will be given to you.*

An Inner Businessman Has Doubts

I have noticed that a part of me—an inner businessman, if you like—still has trouble believing that we own nothing (at least until the end of each year, when he invariably finds that the tax authorities own whatever happens to remain in his business account). This businessman is only interested in the external; he bases his identity on whatever impression he makes on others: what he owns, how much he earns, what kind of car he drives, and how big a house he lives in.

I know this businessman well, and I know where he comes from: it is the part of me that still tries to conquer the world so as to fulfill my mother's ambitions. My mother wanted me to become a doctor—a doctor who would be a member of both Rotary International and Lions International and of course the town council. This doctor would find a wife who would belong to Soroptimist International, at the least, and devote considerable time to charity work. And so I set out to fulfill these aspirations without knowing that they were not mine. I began to study physics and chemistry to be eligible for medical school; for the same purpose, I took private math lessons from a friend of mine.

One term was all I could take; then I used my study loan to buy a motorcycle, looked for a job, and began to drink. This sidestep was instinctive; I did not realize at the time what I had actually done: I had wrenched myself out of my mother's grip and gone my own way. I began to study theology and sought to become qualified as a therapist. I began to build a life of my own and an identity based more on who I really was.

Years later, I had one opportunity to explain my life and choice of career to my mother, to make her see me as the person who I really am. She tried to listen and to understand, but I could see that she understood nothing of what I told her about my life. At that point she was already alcoholic, on medication, and in a violent and catastrophic marriage with her second husband. After I had finished talking, she stated matter-of-factly that she would soon commit suicide; she had already taken care of financial and other matters so that her children would not be left with nothing at all. I was left staring at her; I could not find anything to say.

This heart-to-heart took place in August 1979; I was twenty-nine. The following January my mother did commit suicide. When she sensed that she no longer could base her identity on what I had accomplished, she lost her grip on life irrevocably. Her life was already in such a sad and unfortunate state that she must have felt she had no choice but to end it. In my innermost heart I felt that I had lost a good mother; in spite of everything, she meant a lot to me. At the time, I grieved deeply and said good-bye to her—not realizing that good-byes sometimes last for decades. A part of me still seeks her love by aspiring to what she aspired to.

I have noticed, however, that my inner businessman now has company: an inner monk. This part of me became interested in spirituality and the opportunity within us for a mystical connection with God. This marked the beginning of a longing for something true and real in my life and an extended search for it. An inner burning led me to ask what the meaning of life was and who I really am. I sought the truth—the truth about myself, life, and God.

This journey still continues, and the monk and the businessman contend within me. The monk now has the upper hand; I made him head of the board of directors in my business enterprise, for he knows that I cannot achieve anything through my own struggle. He knows that the more deeply I focus on my actual duties—living in love and doing my work from this context—the freer I am to trust that financial matters will also work out fine. He has proof of this: I started my business amid the great depression of the early nineties and, other than a single newspaper advertisement, I have done nothing to market it. My business is an impossibility—yet it has survived and at times prospered.

life has its own rewards

If we seek entertainment, we should seek rest from work; to savor the pleasure of being entertained, we must first have toiled, struggled, or even suffered pain. When we have worked hard, we have a real appreciation of relaxation and refreshment. The more struggle and pain we have gone through, the easier it is to meet our need for entertainment—sometimes standing still and savoring silence are enough. And if we have *not* toiled or struggled, rest alone does not offer enough enjoyment; we need more powerful entertainment.

Downhill skiing is an occasional hobby of mine, and I must admit that the loudspeakers on the slopes bother and confuse me. Why do we need the music? Because one form of entertainment is not enough? Must we be entertained on top of entertainment so as not to feel bored? Come to think of it, this is not uncommon: we stuff popcorn into our mouths at the movies so as not to feel empty, and newscasts on the radio have background music so that listeners will not become bored and change channels.

Life itself contains enough drama without a soundtrack. It is a drama that we can experience fully if we have the courage to truly live. When we surrender ourselves to life, the need to be constantly entertained disappears.

If we want the approval of our children, we must stop seeking it. This means accepting responsibility for being a parent and having the courage to open the necessary gap between generations. To gain true closeness, we need some distance—trying to be their best pal is too close. Children are free to be children only in the presence of an emotionally mature adult who sets limits, is not intimidated by their outbursts, does not desperately seek approval, and has the courage to await respect when respect is due.

dependency leads to freedom

We find true freedom when we find our complete dependency, when we give up our false sense of self-reliance. We are dependent on others in everything we do; this is a fact of life that we cannot escape. The alcoholic, drug addict, workaholic, and power player try to escape by relying solely on themselves—only to find themselves imprisoned by a lack of love that will eventually destroy them. When we free ourselves from the delusion of having control of our lives, we free ourselves to love. Love is a deep awareness of our dependency on others, a deep realization that we cannot survive alone.

Loving dependency is an absolute value that we should not make relative; if we destroy this value, we become slaves to our desires. Only in loving dependency can we receive what we most deeply need; if we step outside this dependency, our most fundamental human needs are never met. Our deep dependency on others makes us vulnerable, and this vulnerability leads us to our authentic identity. We become ourselves in connection with others.

This leads us to the question of faith and religiousness. True faith originates in vulnerability, in our openness to love. Faith realizes our powerlessness and acknowledges our dependency on others. Religiousness should never abandon this uncertainty, this cry for something beyond our control. God cannot be controlled, not even with religion; God needs to be sovereign, inexplicable, a mystery—only then can we speak to God, only then can we hear God. We can be in connection to God only as deeply as we are willing to acknowledge our vulnerability; a cry from our powerlessness reaches the unreachable. This is the darkness that leads into dazzling light; this is the silence full of thunder.

CHAPTER 5

the less you do, the more you get done

We have created a time characterized by a chronic lack of time. Everybody is in a hurry, rushing to the next appointment or activity, away from the present moment. We seem to feel that we are always doing the wrong thing at the wrong time—that we should already be doing something else. There always is *something else*, something more important that demands our attention.

With this constant lack of time, nobody is present in the here and now, so we are not present to each other. We hurry along, never really meeting anyone. We are not there for each other, which means that we are not there at all. Because none of us *really* sees anyone else—that is, sees beneath the surface to the true self—there is nobody to witness our existence. And without a witness, we cease to exist.

We have invented marvelous machines and devices that were supposed to improve our quality of life. Technology was supposed to free us from tedious routines and save us time—time that we could then devote to what we consider truly important. What happened? Do we have more time? Judging by our unremitting haste, the answer is no. What happened to all that time our great inventions were supposed to save us? Where did it go?

Many people habitually complain about the lack of time as if it were a given—a fact of life that cannot be helped. They wish they had more time, but of course it is out of their hands—there is nothing they can do about it. Is this really the case? Who is responsible for this perpetual time shortage? Is it an immutable fact that simply overpowers us, or have we created it ourselves?

When we take a closer look, we can easily see that the hurry and haste—the sense of time moving faster and faster—does not exist as such. Time still has its own course; it continues to flow at its eternal, steady pace. The essence of time has not suddenly changed during our generation. There still is as much time as there has always been, and it does not flow any faster. Yet we feel that there is less time. Why is that? Are we trying to include too many things in the time that we have on our hands? Are we trying to cram our time chock-full?

Admittedly, it would be easier to think that there is nothing we can do about all our hurry and haste. In that case, we would not have to take responsibility for our choices. But we are responsible for how we use our time. We cannot use constant hurry as an excuse for a lack of time if such a thing does not exist in the first place.

Chronic lack of time always stems from poor choices. Everybody finds the time to do what is important to them. When we make choices in life, we choose what we consider valuable; in other words, our values guide our choices. If we cannot decide what is really valuable to us and what is not, we feel compelled to make as many "valuable" choices as possible. We end up cramming so many "good" things into our lives that we do not have time to deal with the abundance. Why do we make such choices? Does the answer lie in our values? Do our values promote poor choices?

without depth, there is no direction

Superficial values create a superficial life. In a superficial life, there is no room for humanity. As human beings, we have created values that exile us from our own fundamental nature. We no longer know the natural, deliberate rhythm of the human soul. This leads to a soulless life: the soul is left behind, for it cannot keep up with the hasty pace of our existence. When we lose touch with our soul, we lose touch with our deeper nature. This creates a void—a person without an identity, a human being devoid of human qualities.

This feeling of a void is intolerable. We must compensate for it. In the absence of a deep, genuine life, we feverishly produce an imitation of life: a superficial substitute that passes for the real thing. We create an attractive and streamlined identity that has market value—an artificial life that throbs with intensity and seethes with abundance. This compulsion to fill the void produces a set of values marked by rush, frenzy, and performance pressure. Thus we overvalue efficiency. Production and consumption have become the core of our culture, unquestioned ends in themselves.

Devoid of dignity and a true identity, we then measure our value by the impression we make on others. It is all on the surface; what looks good must be good. There is no looking beneath the surface, for we like to believe there is nothing there: no weakness, no incompleteness, no death. All that has been conveniently swept away, declared irrelevant. We are guided not from within, but from without, trying to save travel time on the road to nowhere.

we do not live; we perform life

Our values have created a culture in which people have no rest. The restless person cannot simply be, for being can only spring from a deep conviction that he is loved. Without this assurance, he must struggle to earn the right to exist, to find his place in this world. He does not know that he already has a place. His constant struggle creates great tension—he is not a human being, but a human doing who must convince the world of his value by improving his performance and producing ever more impressive results.

In the Old Testament, God says His name is *I Am* or *the One Who Is*. *Being* is God's core essence. If humanity is an image of God, then being is also *our* core essence. *Being is a serene, restful awareness that we have the right to be who we are—that there is a place for us in this world.* When we have the right to be, we need not struggle. We are convinced we are worthy of love and we are loved. We are at rest with our being, because we are being carried by life.

When a person lacks this awareness, he tries to control life. Feeling that he has no value, he must make himself valuable. Unable to trust that he is loved, he does not give love a chance. He relies solely on himself, becoming overly self-sufficient. Lovelessness fosters unhealthy self-sufficiency: bereft of love, we do not live; we perform life.

man does not trust God; he thinks he is God

When self-sufficiency becomes a survival strategy, the person depending on this strategy actually declares himself God. He trusts only himself and his ability to survive. His sphere of life narrows; he confines himself to a limited life, because he either does not know how to break the boundaries he has created, lacks the courage to do so, or simply sees no point in even trying. He revolves around himself, seeking meaning and significance solely in what he does, trying to control his constricted universe in a godlike manner. He may well think that he is not religious, but he is— very much so. It is a brand-new religion he professes, one so new that it is not yet officially recognized.

In a true, healthy religiousness, God is both love and a person. And these two belong together, for personality can only originate in love. Being born as a person presupposes the presence of love, as it means accepting and acknowledging one's own vulnerability and dependency on others. Becoming a person is a gift we receive from love. Our gratitude to the giver leads us to worship Him, and this fosters a healthy religiousness.

The person who remains out of love's reach does not receive the gift of personality; instead, he creates an identity through achievements and accomplishments—and worships this creation rather than God, the giver of the gift of love that makes each of us a person. Here are the makings of the new religion: an overly self-sufficient person becomes religious without being spiritual. True spirituality involves an awareness of being carried by love, trusting this love, and revealing one's vulnerability in the presence of this love. Without love, religiousness does not acknowledge vulnerability; on the contrary, it may even deny it, having been created in the first place to hide it. It is no surprise, then, that this type of religiousness is characterized by orders and demands rather than by love and grace. It does not worship a loving God; it creates a new god: the false self.

The false self is a compendium of a person's exterior impressions, his carefully constructed facade. When a person's identity is not rooted in love, he must construct a facade convincing enough to impress both himself and others. Many of us spend most of our time tending to our facades, polishing and refining this construction; we seem truly convinced that the impression we make on others is in fact who we are.

This new religion has generated new places of worship: malls and department stores where loudspeakers deliver a sermon—a constant flow of advertisements and special offers on the latest wonder products essential for giving our facade that perfect finish. When we visit one of these sanctuaries, we can almost feel our facade growing stronger. Faced with an infinite array of products designed to improve the impression we make on others, we cannot help but become hyperconscious of our exterior. As we are bombarded with messages emphasizing the importance of our exterior and promoting the essential ingredients for maintaining our artificial identity, we focus on our looks and lose sight of our human worth.

The new religion has scriptures, too: a wide variety of fashion, gossip, and entertainment magazines and tabloids, with articles devoted to the task of constructing and perfecting our facade. We have got to know where the celebrities have been, what they have been up to, what they were wearing, and what they had to say. These magazines reveal to us what these new saints see as sacred.

Here are the new religious icons: the teasers and the screamers. We bow down before them; we must know what the scriptures and icons have to say about the nature of reality today. A beauty queen has forgiven her faithless boyfriend; a movie star, getting married for the fifth time, says he is first and foremost a family man. To those who are striving to mirror the facades of the rich and famous, this is critical information.

Holy meeting places for the followers of this new religion abound on the Internet. The principle is the same as in real life, but the setting is even more sacred, allowing for more creative facades: we are free to put up a splendid, streamlined version of ourselves, equip this facade with attractive attributes, and introduce it into social situations in which it can communicate with other facades.

Nothing is true in these encounters; indeed, that does not seem to be their purpose. No one commits to these virtual relationships, and they have no continuity; before long, the facade is uncovered and must be instantly replaced with artful new lies.

I am busy, therefore I am

In our culture, plagued by a chronic sense of a lack of time, hurry and haste have become the new Black Death. We are in a hurry because we have disconnected doing from being. When we lose touch with being—with the depth of our existence—our values become superficial. We go for fast effects and instant pleasure. We lose the ability to choose what is essential to a good life in the long run. We lose wisdom. Because our choices do not lead to true satisfaction and inner peace, we choose as much as possible—instead of choosing less, but wisely.

When we are disconnected from our deepest selves, we become oblivious to our human worth. Feeling worthless, we can establish our value only through excessive effort, by doing and achieving as much as possible. All our doing and performing becomes an end in itself, such an integral part of our lives that we are no longer able to question it. Surrounded by people who live in the same way, we become blind to the unhealthiness of our rushed, superficial culture; our manic way of life becomes a normal state. We are like alcoholics who deny their addiction; we refuse to see the state we are in, even though it is obvious to those not caught up in it. Other cultures recognize the insane pressure to perform that is inherent in Western culture, but we hold our way of life in such high regard that we expect the rest of the world to eagerly embrace it.

We have created an environment in which there is no room for us as human beings. Superficial values also drive us in our work; the focus is so exclusively on performance and efficiency that we ignore everything else, and by so doing we lose touch with our souls. We lose our depth and identity as we sacrifice our souls on the shrine of efficiency. Production becomes more important than people, and in the process we forget what, why, and for whom we produce.

And what has been produced must, of course, be consumed. Consumption becomes another end in itself, the meaning of modern life. Do we even ask ourselves if we really want to consume everything that we produce? Do we really want to be defined primarily as consumers, or would we like to be seen as something else—perhaps something more human?

When we lose the awareness that love is the deepest, the most profound value in our lives, we start to lead a loveless life. A loveless life means being disconnected from one's own depth—and, in turn, being disconnected from other people. Relationships lose their meaning: there are no longer any real encounters between people, and nobody is truly present to others. The mere chance of two people meeting is being systematically eliminated from our everyday life.

A task as ordinary as buying food illustrates this. Small village and neighborhood stores are becoming extinct. We no longer meet the genial storekeeper with whom we once could discuss our shopping list and wonder about the world. Instead, we have gargantuan markets with endless aisles where we can roam in isolation among strangers, picking up whatever delicacies we fancy.

We no longer value meaningful encounters between people; the goods that we so ardently consume have taken their place. Not that we do not find people useful; we do. We use them in the same way we use things. We have truly mastered the art of networking: we approach encounters with selfish calculation, and deal mainly with people who can bring us some benefit—or who will let us take outright advantage of them.

Working beyond the basic need for a livelihood, we sacrifice our well-being. When we do everything excessively, we get tired. But because we are disconnected from our innermost self, we miss the signals our bodies try to send us. We keep up the good work, the mindless pace. Our tiredness gradually turns into exhaustion—a much deeper state than being tired. Tiredness is physical; exhaustion is psychological. One can recover from tiredness by resting

the less you do, the more you get done

and recharging for a night or a weekend, but a day or two is not enough to recover from exhaustion.

Exhaustion is an inner state that cannot be vanquished without a profound change in one's behavior. Exhaustion is inextricably bound up in our superficial values and the way we devote our lives to them. To change our draining behavior, we must change our values; good intentions or promises are not enough to bring about change. To be able to choose differently, we must deeply desire to change our lives. Most of us do not change until we have no other option but to change—until our lives are too painful not to change.

being begins with facing ourselves

The essence of efficiency is producing the results we want with the smallest possible expenditure of time and energy. How can we learn to do less and, at the same time, actually achieve more? Though it may sound impossible, it can be done—if what we do is anchored in our depth. This means beginning to let our *being* direct what we do and how we do it. Remember: *being is a serene, restful awareness that we have the right to be who we are—that there is a place for us in this world.* Being becomes the place in which doing happens. We soon discover that in this state of rest, efficiency blossoms.

How can we reach this serene state that sounds too good to be true? We find rest when we face what makes us restless. The fundamental cause of restlessness is invariably the same: there is something within us that we have not faced, with which we have not yet come to terms. If the loss of an authentic self is the real reason behind our chronic exhaustion, then to recover we must reconnect with our true being. We find rest when we face our true selves.

Facing ourselves means facing our inner depths. Within each of us there is an inner personality, an inner child utterly lacking in self-deception. There lies our authenticity, our genuineness; there we are what we really are. In our innermost self, we are each real and true. This is a characteristic we share with all creation. Focus your attention on birds or butterflies; you can sense their restfulness. A bird does not struggle to be something other than what it is. A butterfly is a butterfly, and a worm is a worm. The grass on the ground is content with what it is. The cloud in the sky does not repine; it continues to roam the skies. Dogs are completely sincere, lacking all pretense—they never wag their tails with feigned enthusiasm.

This authenticity, this sincerity is inherent in all creation—including humans. We alone have lost touch with our natural restfulness, our ability to be. But we can rediscover this ability, if we are willing to face and acknowledge what is true within us.

love lights our way into our inner darkness

Jesus said that the truth will make us free. I believe it is safe to assume that the truth he spoke about also refers to the subjective truth inside us all: the truth about ourselves. Knowing who we are makes us free, and this truth is not merely an abstract philosophical concept.

Jesus could also have said that the truth may make us very uncomfortable; in fact, it will make us hurt. It is not particularly pleasant to face one's own untruth. When our skeletons come clattering out of the closet, we must face our insecurity and our facades.

This is why no one enters therapy just for the fun of it. People usually start therapy when they have tried everything else, when they are running out of options. We begin to change only when it becomes too painful not to change; pain and suffering impel us to personal growth and development. Only by facing this pain can we finally connect with our deepest self.

But pain is not, in and of itself, propitious, for it can just as easily lead to self-destruction. We must also have love, for only those surrounded by love can face their depth. Love shields us when we enter the insecurity within. Love, too, is not an abstract concept, nor does it refer to philosophical truths, sentimentality, or beautiful thoughts. To be surrounded by love means having someone available to us, really present, someone with a loving attitude toward us. This person is willing to stand by us and also knows how to be firm, if need be. In fact, true love is always firm; it is the kind of love that does not overlook the truth, even if the truth hurts. Love never evades pain and suffering, for it is well aware of their value. Love may not always feel nice—but its intentions are never hurtful.

To face the insecurity within us, we must not be alone. We cannot acknowledge our weakness without an enlightened witness who knows where we are headed and will see us all the way through our journey. This companion can be a therapist, a counselor, a spouse, a friend, or a self-help group; it can be a book or an audiotape, which provides a form of human interaction; or it can be any combination of these.

once mistreated, we seek mistreatment

Finding love and support is especially difficult for anyone who was not loved as a child. Living in lovelessness inflicts deep wounds upon children. However, as children we are not aware of these wounds. If a child lives in an environment in which she is mistreated, abused, and abandoned, the child becomes accustomed to it. Children living in such circumstances do not comprehend that they are being mistreated; instead, they grow to believe there is something wrong with them. Children cannot critically evaluate their mother's or father's parenting skills, but they do perceive their own value according to the way they are treated. The child is so totally dependent on her parents that she would sooner forsake her true inner feelings than renounce her parents. This creates infantile loyalty, a characteristic typical of children: the child takes responsibility for being mistreated. She feels she is a bad person, instead of realizing that her parents are responsible for treating her badly and without love.

Little by little, the child's personality becomes bound with shame. When our personalities are tangled with shame, we carry the consequences of lovelessness within us, unable to see the inner wounds inflicted there. We do not know that we missed out on something significant—something essential—in our childhood. Our deep inner wounds remain hidden because we don't perceive ourselves as having been mistreated and deprived of a happy childhood.

If our personality is shame-bound, we resist and repel love—by, for example, mistrusting others and the sincerity of their love. We reject reliable and loving people and seek out the company of those who mistreat us. In their company, we feel safe in a strange but familiar way.

the less you do, the more you get done

we move from outer to inner success

When we finally receive love from others, we gradually begin to adopt a loving, caring, compassionate attitude toward ourselves. Our values deepen, becoming human. That is, we begin to take seriously the task of protecting our true personality—the unique and authentic personality that is in our innermost self.

With the deepening of our values, we may also begin to see the hollowness behind our striving for outward success and admiration. When our true selves begin to be born from within, we no longer need a showy exterior to convince others—or ourselves—that we exist. The feeling of life that comes from within us is so strong that we gradually lose interest in fabricating a facade. We no longer measure our success externally—we measure it internally. This inner success means that our life is in harmony with our true personality.

"Do I have the kind of job that I really want? Do I want to be in this marriage? Does this house that I live in truly feel like it is mine? Am I living my own life or a life defined by others?" These are questions that arise as we begin to truly settle into the life that was meant to be ours.

As our values deepen, we begin to really want something instead of merely drifting into different things. Establishing our own free will is an important sign that we have reconnected with our authentic self. When we want something other than what our culture considers valuable—no longer focusing solely on surface issues or worshiping performance—we suddenly find ourselves at odds with our environment. In this situation, then, will we want change deeply enough to bring it about—or will our changes be limited to mere plans and good intentions?

a deep life does not just happen— it must be chosen

When our values deepen, one of the first questions we face is the question of time. To listen to our deepest truths and take our true self seriously, we must learn how to be present—*to* ourselves and *within* ourselves. People who live in a chronic rush are never present to themselves, or others, and are never attentive to what is going on within. We cannot live a deep life until we take responsibility for our busyness. We have to understand that constant hurry is not something that happens to us; it is something we create through the choices we make. We are responsible for our harried way of life. In turn, we can create a more deliberate, unhurried life by choosing differently. A deliberate, unhurried life is not predestined; it is not a fate that happens to fall on some of us but not on others. It is clearly a choice.

Everyone who enters a process of growth and change must answer the question "Do you want to be healed?" Do you want to face your insecurities and live creatively and with love? A deep life must become a way of life to which we are committed. We have to want it so much that we are willing to give up something else.

Today Is a Good Day to Change

Wanting to be healed means reserving time to take the necessary steps to initiate and promote personal growth. We must allow time for discovering our true personality and maintaining a deep life. This may sound easy and self-evident, but in practice it is anything but. It is far from certain that we actually want to recover, even though we say we do, for there is often a certain safety in sickness. Let me give an example from my own life.

Years ago, when I decided I was going to give up smoking, I found the process had definite phases. First, I had to suffer from my smoking habit to such a degree that it became an everyday pain that lasted for years. This made me *begin* to quit. This first phase involved talking about quitting and planning to do it. I made promises and tried many different tactics. Because it is common knowledge that kicking the cigarette habit is fiendishly hard to do, I thought I would not be able to do it right away; I would have to wait for a more convenient time. That time was always tomorrow, or a time much further in the future—certainly not today.

I knew trying to quit would ruin my holidays, so I decided to quit in August, after my summer vacation. Come August, I was not yet thoroughly prepared, so I decided to quit the following week. After the week had passed, I decided to quit the following day, because on that particular day I had already smoked a few cigarettes. It would be easier to quit, I thought, if I could start with a clean slate.

This phase took several years.

The next phase was to *quit quitting*. I had to realize that there would be no end to my smoking habit unless I put an end to it. Mere intentions or solemn plans were not enough. Quitting was impossible as long as I put a cigarette in my mouth and lit the end.

This realization led me to the third phase of the process: *quitting*. This phase was about not lighting a cigarette. It was also about realizing that it would not be the least bit easier tomorrow than it was today. Today is a good time to quit. Amazingly simple! Nonetheless, it took me years to realize this.

Taking responsibility for how we use our time is a process with fairly similar phases. First, there are plans and intentions to lead an unhurried life. We may be motivated by exhaustion or burnout, in other words, pain and suffering. This phase includes talking about the virtues of a leisurely life at every opportunity. People may even write books or give lectures about the subject, or become consultants who teach others how to live so that they do not have to make changes in their own lives. They give others the impression that they are about to leave the rat race and make radical changes in their way of life. They make and break all kinds of promises. Then they feel shamed and guilty, which spurs them to renewed plans, grand intentions, and new promises.

In this phase, you may get a new job or a new hobby. You acquire a new calendar or a time management system that you expect will work miracles. With great determination, you mark time for family, friends, and spouse. When it comes down to the crunch, though, these plans are abandoned. The boss asks if you would like to be involved in an important project. You really do not have the time, so you make time by erasing family and friends from the pages of your calendar. You think you will make it up to them someday by giving up something else in their favor, but it never happens. You never take that step from good intentions to real action.

Being Rejected May Be a Necessary Risk

Taking real action hinges on wanting something deeply enough—wanting it so much that you are willing to face the risk of being rejected, for example, in the workplace. Ultimately, this means you are willing to risk being fired. This may sound extreme, but it is important to remember that you may well find yourself in a situation in which you must choose between life and death—whether you want to leave and get on with your real life, or stay and become afflicted with a chronic illness that could prove fatal. Hanging on to a job is a cold comfort if you are unable to work—or six feet under.

This reminds me of a time when I was working as a counselor at an addiction treatment center. My duties at the center were interesting—even groundbreaking—and I was entrusted with great responsibility. I enjoyed this job because I was able to fully employ my creativity.

But gradually I began to experience strange symptoms. I felt dizzy; the world was spinning. I had these spells particularly in the morning. I recall that when the symptoms were at their strongest, shortly before a vacation, when walking to work I had to lean on walls for support. I was examined, but the doctor found nothing unusual; however, the symptoms became worse. Then, during my vacation, the symptoms disappeared in a few weeks, for good, I thought. But no—they returned on the day I returned to work, and this forced me to stop and think. I consulted a physiotherapist, who thought that the extreme tension in my neck muscles could cause the dizzy spells. Physiotherapy alleviated the symptoms somewhat, but not completely.

After various stages of pain, I began to realize that these symptoms were connected to one of my coworkers, who had managed to draw me into his inner drama. I had not noticed that this person was ambitious for power and clearly displayed narcissistic characteristics; instead, I had routinely blamed myself for the problems in our communication. I had tried to please my coworker as best I could, be compliant and do things better. But when I began to discern the pattern, I had no choice but to set boundaries.

This caused a serious conflict that spread throughout the organization. I could not keep silent and bear the blame; instead,

I requested an appointment with the director of the board and demanded that the issue be addressed—otherwise I would give notice. The director appeared very understanding; he was aware of the problem and had been expecting me to bring it up sooner or later. He promised a reorganization and restored peace at work, but I somehow sensed that these were only placating words; he would not be able to untangle the snarl of problems at this workplace. So I gave an ultimatum: if the changes were not pursued within two months, I would resign.

I found defending myself immensely difficult and threatening. And to make matters even more stressful, we had three little children, I was up to my ears in debt after building a house with my family, and I was the only family member with an income.

I resigned from my job. That was seventeen years ago; the dizzy spells disappeared and have not returned since. Other aspects of my life also sorted themselves out with time: I opened a private practice and gained enough business to support my family and reduce my debt. I can now see that my body had an understanding of which my mind was not aware; the dizzy spells were signals of this understanding. If we ignore the signals that the body sends, the message will gradually grow so powerful that we cannot help hearing it.

Choosing a deep life is a process that requires wanting a change so much that your choices and actions actually begin to change. If you want a deep life, you begin to choose healthy unhurriedness, even though this choice may clash with your environment and cause conflict. Making such a change also leads to conflict within—to inner warfare in which one part of you wants peace and quiet and the other part tries to pull you back into that familiar hustle and bustle of hectic activity. However, something new has already been born: a loving attitude toward yourself, an ability to take your true self seriously. Now you want to take good care of yourself, for you are no longer willing to overlook what is precious and real within.

silence holds traces of the past

When we begin to limit the rush of hectic activity outside ourselves, we begin to discern what is inside us. We cannot see what is within until we consciously choose to stop and look. When we turn our vision inward, in times of silence, we begin to see things that we should have seen long before.

I have witnessed this many a time in my therapeutic work. When a person regularly sets aside time to explore his inner depths, eliminating external disturbances, and enters a time and place specifically reserved for what is within, he sends his inner issues a signal that he now considers them important and will focus his attention on them. These buried issues are now uncovered; they begin to stir, starting a process. In this process, the person faces all the experiences and events in his life that he has not yet processed.

Inside each of us are traces of what we have left behind, waiting for our attention. These traces may be left by experiences whose meaning and dynamics we did not understand, experiences we simply endured, never able to process them in any way. We may harbor painful feelings, such as grief, anger, and hurt or insecurity and fear. If we have never stopped to listen to and discern the true meaning of these experiences, then like foreign bodies they will bind our energy.

When we consciously turn our attention within, to these inner traces of our past, we actually seek our way to our true self, to everything that we once abandoned. We no longer want to participate in abandoning parts of ourselves. Instead we embrace a loving attitude toward ourselves, which leads to recovery and integration. Love makes us whole by bringing us face to face with our brokenness, our incompleteness. And we become vulnerable, which often hurts. Maybe this is the real reason behind our constant hurry: we are making sure that we never have to face what could make us hurt.

silence holds intimations of what is to come

The silence within us not only holds traces of our past, but it also seems to hint at the future direction of our growth. The origins of what we will be are there—we are already on our way to a destination of which we are not yet aware. If we learn to stop and listen to the silence within, we may sense intimations of our future. These hints reflect our fears and dreams, what we are afraid of and, at the same time, wish for. What does this mean?

Our true personalities can only be born to the extent that we are seen and heard. We learn to know ourselves through others; we are born the way others see us. When, for example, a child's sadness is acknowledged, the child does not have to hide it inside. He is allowed to feel it, and it becomes integrated as one of the many features of his personality.

Inside us all, there is much that has not yet been seen or heard, so we are not yet all that we could be. The undiscovered aspects of ourselves strive to emerge in many ways, responding to our innate ability to be born as our authentic selves. This ability is also known by another name: creativity. Creativity is a characteristic of the Creator, manifested in the entirety of His work. In creation, everything is about change, motion, and growth. In order for us to live—not to merely exist—we too must change, move, and grow.

Our dreams and wishes are part of the creative work in motion within us. If we venture to listen to our dreams, they can tell us what we will become in the future. Our dreams invite us to be something new and different—so we may feel intimidated by what we wish for. What we dream of, and fear, is part of the future already within us. For us to step into our future—into where we are more real, more ourselves—we need courage and faith. We must believe in the significance of our dreams; we must take them so seriously that we give them our full attention. Our dreams are an invitation to a courageous life—to really being alive instead of merely surviving or playing it safe.

The greatest dream a human being can have is that of being loved. It is also the most dangerous, because if we really believe that we are loved, life changes radically: we learn to trust, to release our life into bigger hands. We no longer cling to secure positions; instead, we start to take life as it comes.

Love invites us to surrender, love invites us to trust, and therefore love leads us to change—to birth the person deep within us.

when we trust, we find true efficiency in rest

When we speak of rest and silence, the words are often misunderstood. They do not mean passiveness and inactivity. On the contrary, *true rest is profound activity*. The more we are at rest in our being, the more alert and prepared we are to act. In the Old Testament, Isaiah says: "In quietness and trust is your strength"—which is to say that our real strength is not in hectic, overheated activity but in calm trust. Why is this, and what does it mean?

To live in calm trust means to gain an ability to listen to ourselves, an ability so profound that, in our inner depths, we begin to sense a connection with something greater than ourselves. The more we listen to these depths, the more this listening becomes a dialogue.

A dialogue is more than a monologue. In a monologue, one person speaks but no one answers. In a dialogue, one person speaks and somebody answers. It can even be said that in a dialogue somebody speaks and we listen. The deeper our awareness of our inner dialogue, the more we experience being carried. We notice that, even in situations that seem insurmountable and impossible, we are, nevertheless, carried through them. The more profoundly we realize this, the more we begin to trust the other party in this dialogue, the party whose presence we sense within: God. *When we live in a conscious connection with God, we gradually become convinced, at a deep emotional level, that we are being carried. This is trust.*

When this trust deepens, we gradually dare to trust God more than we trust our own activity. We stop struggling to live on our own; instead, we rest.

However, rest requires both humility and courage. We cannot rest unless we realize that our own strength is not enough, that our resources are limited. We rarely gain this understanding until we have depleted ourselves. This is by no means a pleasant experience, but it is essential because it makes us humble. Humility keeps us conscious; without it, we are unaware of our limits.

Why do we need courage to be able to rest? We live in a culture that overrates performance and efficiency. It is not easy to explain or defend the importance of being still. If we want to relinquish our excessive activity and obsessive need to control, we often must act against what is expected of us. We need courage to protect ourselves when all around us are willing to sacrifice their health to an intolerable workload.

When we reconnect with our inner depth, we begin to be directed from within, from the core of our being. Everything we do is colored by what we learn from within. We no longer do things in an effort to establish an impressive identity; we do things because we *have* an authentic identity. This releases all that energy that we have been wasting in our feverish effort to make a good impression, to convince others of our great value, measured in terms of performance. We are at rest in what we do, for we are at rest in our true selves.

Creativity means that your true self, your authentic personality, is present in everything you do, imbuing it with your own unique color and voice. This leads, in turn, to a joy of work. My grandmother had a towel embroidered with these words: *Joy of work is a gift from God*. I used to look at it when I was a small boy, but I did not pay much attention to the saying; I did not understand it. I only thought that it testified to my grandmother's religiousness.

But now I begin to see how great a secret was revealed in that simple embroidery.

Perhaps we could rephrase it to better correspond to the reality of our time. In the process, the phrase loses its poetic simplicity, but it becomes more understandable in modern terms:

When we are directed from within, from deep spiritual values, we make our peace with the insecurity inherent in life. We have the courage to be present, as an authentic personality, in everything that we do. Thus, in everything we do we create something new and experience joy.

When our personality colors our work, we no longer feel compelled to always do the same things in the same way. We are no longer directed by fear; avoiding mistakes is no longer a priority. Instead, we feel a natural, healthy drive to create something new. Again, despite our newly found inner security, creating something new requires courage in the face of vulnerability. When we let our personality show in what we do, we take a risk—after all, creativity means thinking and doing things in a new way, defying existing patterns, structures, and conventions. For those who cling to how things *should* be, insecurity prevents them from taking such a risk. True creativity always includes an element of heroism.

Combined with courage, restfulness gives rise to a paradoxical efficiency: we do less and accomplish more. This is the fifth paradox we meet on our journey: *The less you do, the more you get done.*

We do less when we are at rest in our being and directed from deep within. Doing a great deal is no longer an end in itself—we choose the right things to do because we have better judgment about our true selves and the future that is best for us. We feel safe within, which leads to a new kind of courage: the courage to be present as our true selves in everything we do. We find new, creative solutions, which leads to increased efficiency—efficiency gained from being at rest.

CHAPTER 6

only alone can we be together

Nowadays the breakup of a marriage has become the rule rather than the exception. We find it harder and harder to make this union last. As a result, we seem to be losing the courage to enter into matrimony. We prefer other arrangements because they are easier to get out of.

What is it that makes it so hard for us to establish enduring bonds and stay in a relationship? In countless cases, the marriage fails because one partner is unable to respect the other as an individual. This respect involves acknowledging, appreciating, and giving space to the partner's autonomy.

Love fosters and encourages the individual personality. It strives to create an atmosphere in which each partner's true self can come into existence and we can experience and express the full depth of our personalities. Love can only thrive in a relationship where this respect for the other's personhood—his or her integrity and autonomy—is actualized. In such a relationship, we become seen as the people we really are.

If we cannot appreciate a partner's autonomy, we fail or refuse to see the partner's true self. Our perception is distorted by unmet needs we still carry from childhood or adolescence—needs that have to do with our parents. We cannot reasonably expect our partner to fulfill these needs.

Still, our unmet childhood needs do not lose intensity or disappear over time. They brood inside us, real and compelling. They demand satisfaction. Our past begins to sabotage our present with unrealistic expectations, no longer recognized as the needs of the child of long ago. In the present, these needs turn into unreasonable demands that we usually make of those closest to us—most often a spouse. We may defy personal boundaries, not respecting our significant other as a separate, adult individual. We burden them with inappropriate responsibility, expecting them to vanquish our distress. Instead of joining our spouse in equal partnership, we exploit the relationship for our own purposes. This takes many forms; we can, for example, desperately cling to a spouse and expect him or her to provide us with a level of safety and protection that no adult can be expected to provide for another.

Life is unsafe. As children, we have a right to expect the adults around us to provide shelter and protection. But as we enter adulthood we must gradually learn to face, on our own, the unpredictability and insecurity inherent in life. Some adults are unwilling to accept this responsibility; they cling to others and refuse to grow, expecting others to take the adult role in their stead. They blame others for their hardships and expect others to assume responsibility for their distress. In so doing, they behave like little children, never needing to give anything or take others into account. They admit no responsibilities; they recognize only their entitlement.

Life is a responsibility that we cannot delegate. When we become adults we must stop expecting others to mother or father us; we must become our own parents. We must grow up and become individuals willing to take responsibility for our lives and, as needed, to confront our past.

our past is the third wheel in our relationships

Both of the following examples show how unresolved issues of the past prevent us from living fully in the present. We are unable to see our partners as they really are; instead, we see an image distorted by our past needs. Unconsciously living in the past and reliving it at a symbolic level has become our "normal" state of being. But in a relationship, this inevitably causes problems. Each partner feels unhappy and blames the other for his or her misery. Each tries to make the other change. Held prisoner by their past, both partners are unable to grow.

"Where Are You, Strong Woman? I Am Here, Your Feeble Fellow."

A person who has decided not to grow up declines all responsibility. He finds someone—in most cases, a spouse—who is willing to take more than her fair share of responsibility. How does he do it?

He does it instinctively. He sends out subconscious signals that can be read by those who fit his requirements. For example, a man can signal helplessness in a way that reveals he is looking for a

only alone can we be together

woman who is willing to take care of him and accept the responsibilities of a mother. If interpreted, these secret signals could, for example, read something like this: "Where are you, strong and powerful woman? I am here, your weak, helpless fellow, your man who will always need you and depend on you! I want you to take responsibility for me. I need you because I do not want to grow up. I need you to become my mother. Take me under your wing!"

On the subconscious level, these secret signals appeal to a woman who is looking for someone to take care of. She may already have a long history of taking care of others, starting in early childhood with her mother or father. Taking care of others has become an integral part of her identity. She can connect with other people only by being the one on whom they depend. If she is, first and foremost, perceived as someone who is always there to help and understand others, she has also learned to see herself in this way. She lacks the ability to take herself into consideration, to pay attention to her own needs. Instead, she concentrates on others, always concerned for their well-being, attuned to their needs at the expense of her own.

When any woman receives signals sent by a helpless man, alarm bells should go off. The selfless woman does not hear the bells, however—or if she does, she mistakes them for wedding bells. She falls in love instantly. She feels she has finally met the love of her life. But this man and woman are not able to join each other in equal partnership as adult individuals. Instead, their unresolved past issues distort the ways in which they see each other. Subconsciously, their past sabotages their present. They do not fall in love with each other; they fall for the hope of finally getting their childhood needs met.

"Where Are You, Weak One? Come Here So I Can Control You."

Let us take another example: A woman grows up unable to identify with her mother. The mother may reject her daughter, seeing her as a threatening competitor. It may be that the mother has never come to terms with her womanhood, never learned to value her femininity. She may be a victim of childhood sexual abuse who has never had the chance to work through these painful experiences. She has had no other choice but to suppress all memories and feelings connected with the abuse. Therefore she is unaware of the effect the abuse still has on her sexuality. She does not like the woman within her, so she dislikes the woman she sees in her daughter. She is unable to cherish her daughter; she does not enjoy being close to her, and she rarely touches her, holds her, or shows her affection. She may take good care of her daughter, but only out of a sense of duty. Because she harbors feelings of guilt for her inability to delight in her child, she tries to be the perfect mother, doing everything "by the book," but still she remains distant from her own child. Masked by a veneer of perfection, however, the distance between mother and daughter goes unnoticed.

The daughter has no opportunity to learn from her mother what it is to be a woman. Without closeness, she cannot find in her mother the feminine counterpart she needs to connect with and emulate. She remains out of touch with her womanhood, unable to love and respect the woman within herself, because her mother has ignored and rejected that woman.

At the same time, the father may communicate through his behavior that he does not respect his wife. The parents' relationship may be characterized by a lack of true closeness, which affects the parents' emotional well-being. The father takes out his anger and frustration on his wife. He lets her know, in countless ways, how defective, flawed, and inferior he finds her. It may be that the father has not acknowledged the weakness within him; instead, he has learned to despise it. He may well regard femininity as a weakness, so he attacks the woman in his wife, treating her with the same disrespect he feels toward his own weakness. In so doing, he teaches his daughter to disrespect herself. The daughter reads her own value as a woman in the signals the father sends to the mother with his criticism and contempt. The daughter learns that she has no value.

In order to gain self-confidence and self-respect, the daughter has no choice but to identify with her father. She does not feel like a woman, but she knows that she is not a man either. She feels compelled to compensate for her lack of manhood by acting like a man as best she can. Disconnected from her womanhood, she struggles in her lack of manhood. She feels close to her father; with his encouragement, she may even transfer all her love from her mother to him and join with him in rejecting his wife. In despising her mother, the daughter also learns to despise herself as a woman.

A woman who is in harmony with her femininity is aware of her worth as a woman; to her, femininity is a natural state of being. It is not a threat or a defect for which she need compensate. She enjoys living with a man; she is on an equal footing with her husband, even though she is different from him. Their equality is founded on their respect for each other's true identities—their differences as well as their commonalities.

When the daughter in our example—who is unable to identify with her mother and lacks a positive model of healthy womanhood—

grows up, she becomes what is sometimes referred to as a "phallic woman" in psychoanalytical theory. By imitating her father's ruthless behaviors, she tries to compensate for not being a man—the only gender she believes is worthy of value and admiration. Unable to join a man in equal partnership as a woman, she seeks out a spouse who will allow himself to be controlled and ordered around. Their relationship is marked by an ongoing power struggle, manifested in constant conflict and argument. The woman feels that she must be dominant—dominant enough to suppress her masculine counterpart in her man in an effort to avoid facing her femininity.

In this relationship, there can be no true intimacy, for the man and the woman are not present to each other as a man and a woman. They both feel an emptiness and unease in their relationship because their needs are not met. In the throes of their power struggle, they blame each other for their distress. This makes their search for intimacy even more difficult.

In his wife's presence, the man feels disheartened in a way that he cannot rationally explain. As long as he is willing to take the role of the miserable man, both man and woman avoid facing their pain. But if the man starts to question his role in the relationship and refuses to be defined by his wife, he creates a crisis in the relationship. This crisis can lead to growth—leaving each partner no choice but to face and address their pain. Otherwise, they may be facing divorce.

we cannot see others unless we first see ourselves

It is possible to thrive in a relationship only when mutual respect prevails; in other words, when both partners see each other as they really are. Without this respect, the relationship is not about joining with the other; it is about using the other. Joining is not possible until there is someone who can join, until both partners are connected with their authentic selves. We must realize our own true personalities before we can recognize and respect the personalities of others. And so we consider our sixth paradox: *Only alone can we be together.*

If we are not aware of our past, we inevitably continue to dwell in it. If we are imprisoned by our personal past, our authentic personalities cannot be born. Distorting the way we see ourselves, our past distorts our perceptions of others. To see others as they really are, we must first truly see ourselves—and to see ourselves, we must remove the obstacles that block our vision. We must face our past and become aware of what lies therein.

When we face our past, we accept responsibility for ourselves. This means that we stop imposing our unresolved issues on others. We do not hold friends, coworkers, neighbors, and the person who cut us off in traffic responsible for our misery—and we do not expect that life would change for the better if only our partner would be willing to change.

Taking responsibility for ourselves requires acknowledging our own imperfection and incompleteness. As long as we are blind to our shortcomings and deny our need to grow, we are tempted to hold our partner responsible for our unhappiness. But we often do not admit to our pain until it hurts enough; we are not willing to acknowledge it until it becomes too intense to avoid or ignore.

Growth is not possible as long as we expect others to shoulder the burden of our pain. Let us return to our example of the ruthless woman and her meek and miserable husband. If the man continues to assume his present role in their relationship, his wife has no real reason to face her problems; her illusions of power and control are not threatened in any way. And the man does not grow aware that he is shouldering someone else's pain until he truly sees himself.

Facing one's pain is by no means a pleasant experience. It is far more convenient to blame another than to face our own incompleteness. But acknowledging our own incompleteness is the only way we can learn to respect others. Until we do so, our relationships lack true intimacy and we are unable to join our significant other in equal partnership.

A lack of respect for others usually indicates superficial self-knowledge. The less well we know ourselves, the more compelled we feel to criticize, judge, and condemn others. As the New Testament puts it, we see the speck in our neighbor's eye, but we do not see the log in our own eye. We criticize and condemn others to avoid facing our weakness. In despising others, we really despise what we are unwilling to acknowledge within us. Our judgment of others actually says more about us than about those we hold in contempt. The greater the evil we want to avoid within, the more intense our need to condemn others. The more deeply we get to know ourselves, the better able we are to respect others.

only alone can we be together

love can only live in total freedom

True love can only live in total freedom. Total freedom prevails in a relationship in which both partners are able to love each other unconditionally, without setting any requirements or preconditions for their love. Love cannot be demanded, and it is impossible to love anyone out of duty. But a person who refuses to grow up makes demands of love. He demands that his partner parent him so that he can remain a child and not have to take responsibility for his own life.

Only when we take responsibility for our own life are we capable of true love. We are willing to take responsibility for our troubles; we do not try to pawn them off on others. We are aware of our past and how it affects our present, and if we are not always aware, we are always open to self-examination. We do not feel comfortable blaming others.

We also know that we are responsible for our own emotional well-being. If we are treated with disrespect in a relationship, we do not complain about the situation for years on end—we try to do something about it. We realize that it is impossible to make another person change, so we do not try to do so. We also understand that it is our responsibility to let our partner know if we are not feeling well in the relationship. Furthermore, we are aware that we cannot force personal growth in our partner; both people have the right to make their own choices. This does not mean, of course, that we should resign ourselves to being treated with disrespect. It would be a disservice to both partners if both did not protect themselves against such behavior. If one partner persistently refuses to take personal responsibility, divorce may be a healthier choice than mute, stoic acceptance.

Many people, however, reconcile themselves to mistreatment because their fears prevent them from leaving a bad relationship. They are afraid to be alone. Their unresolved fears of rejection can be so intense that they are willing to stay in the worst of relationships. They cling to their abusive partner, willing to endure anything as long as they do not have to face life on their own. They are unwilling to face their loneliness until they feel so wretched, miserable, and suffocated that they have absolutely no choice but to leave the relationship.

In this situation, however, facing potential loneliness is the only path to growth. Leaving an abusive relationship requires positive anger—a power that enables us to break away from mistreatment. But if our fear of abandonment prevents us from exercising this power, it turns inward and gradually turns into bitterness, depression, hatred, and malevolence.

we can share others' pain, but we cannot take it away from them

It feels good to be around those who take responsibility for their feelings. They are not surrounded by a minefield in which we must carefully watch every step. Such a minefield surrounds those who have important issues in their personal past that they have not faced and worked through. Around these people, we must keep up our guard so as not to step on an emotional mine. One wrong move, one wrong word can cause an explosion.

Those who have acknowledged their past and taken responsibility for their feelings are more predictable. Their reactions are appropriate, reasonable, and understandable; in other words, they react like an adult.

When we take responsibility for our own life we are able to have a close relationship with another person without trying to live his life for him. We respect the other person and keep a respectful distance from the core of his being—a place that is private and sacred. We know that being close to somebody means sharing her pain and suffering; however, it does not mean trying to take it away from her. If we respect another person, we do not meddle in her life, driven by a self-righteous need to rescue, help, or heal her. We realize that it is impossible for us to know what is right for someone else and what is not. Even God does not try to force His presence if not invited.

Pain, agony, and suffering encourage growth. When we face our pain, at least some of it, we are aware of this. Thus, we do not try to free another person from his pain; instead, we allow him to face it and work through it. But we stay by his side, offering compassion and support.

We often mistake our taking responsibility for others for simply helping them. We step in and take over—we start living their life for them. We feel the need to protect them from whatever we think they need to be protected from, ignoring that it might be us. We avoid telling them the truth, in case it might hurt their feelings. We do not seem to understand that while the truth can be painful, ultimately it does not harm anyone; on the contrary, it makes us free.

Our responsibility is to tell the truth. Of course, this does not give us the right to violate others by flinging a painful "truth" in their face. The truth is always defined by love; it lacks any harmful intention. If we are open to our own pain we are aware of this, so we are not afraid to tell someone else truths that he may not necessarily want to hear. We are not responsible for how the other person reacts to the truth.

Most often, it is our fears that prevent us from telling the truth as we understand it—to our spouse, for example. We are afraid of our partner's reactions—especially her anger—and we are afraid of rejection. We tiptoe around our partner, careful not to step on an emotional mine. We protect her from ourselves. In avoiding conflict at any cost, we deprive the relationship of love, for honest conflict paves the way to true intimacy. When we "protect" our partner from our feelings, we are actually manipulating him. We are not honest; instead of showing our true colors, we color the truth. We hide our true personality and beliefs inside a more presentable package, one that we think will be more to our partner's liking. In so doing, we control our partner's reactions, not allowing him to think for himself.

When we protect our partner in this way, we ignore and abandon our true self. We wander further and further from our truth, losing our way in manipulation. If one partner controls the other with blame, guilt, or anger, the intimidated partner gradually loses his or her identity. If we lose our identity, we are no longer capable of love, for love is an emotion that only a genuine personality can convey.

When we live with another person instead of living for him or her, we feel no need to rescue our partner from anything. We realize that we cannot change her or make demands on her. There is no need to "help" or advise her, no need to cling to her, no need to make decisions for her or protect her from the truth. But there is no need to abandon her, either. We can share our humanity with her. We can stand by her and wonder at the world with her. We can become her co-wonderer, sharing the journey of discovery and adventure with her. When there is no need to play God, we are free to be human: wonderers, seekers on the verge of great discoveries.

no is a sacred word

When we take responsibility for our life and stand on our own two feet, we dare to say no. *No* is a sacred word. On the outside, it may appear small and undramatic, but it is loaded with immense power.

When we say no, we take a great risk of being abandoned. Others may not regard us as nice and pleasant. They may even think that we are wrong. For this reason, we must be able to rely on something within us when others deny us their support or encouragement. This something within is our identity, the core of our being. If we have the courage to say no, we express—not only to others, but also to ourselves—our belief in something more important than pleasing others. Here, again, we are living dangerously, living creatively.

This creative process honors our true identity. If we always compromise to gain acceptance, we abandon our true selves. But if we find safety within ourselves, we find the courage to say no and remain loyal to our core being.

When we feel able to say no, we stop demanding love from others. Instead, we begin seeking love inside ourselves, directing our questions to the depths of our being: Is there anything in life I can depend upon? Is there a lap on which I can rest? Does life mean merely being at the mercy of nameless powers of chaos, or does everything have a meaning? In other words, we ask, is there a God?

The question about God is, in fact, a question about love—for it really makes no difference whether there is a God if that God is not a loving God. Thus life's greatest question is not, is there a God? but, is there a loving God?

Being born as a person means entering solitude, accepting that we are separate from all others. We must have the courage to stand alone, trusting that we are loved. It is impossible for us to find our true identity until we experience being loved. Only then do we learn who we are and become able to profoundly join others.

CHAPTER 7
only together can we be alone

Man was created to live in communion with others. Each of us needs an emotionally close community in which we can become and be ourselves. Through communion we are nurtured with the emotional food we must have to grow as human beings.

The opposite of isolation, communion, means profound interaction: exposing our vulnerabilities to others, letting them enter our most secret and carefully guarded areas. Our identity is formed in loving and truthful interaction with others. In this interaction we also grow to our proper size. We get a healthy sense of proportion—an understanding of what we are capable of on our own and when we need the help of others. In other words, communion protects us against excessive self-sufficiency.

Why would we need to be protected from self-sufficiency? In our culture this quality is generally considered to be a virtue—indeed, a necessity. However, I draw a crucial distinction between self-sufficiency and taking responsibility for one's life. When I speak of excessive or unhealthy self-sufficiency, I refer to our striving to take complete care of ourselves because we are unable to trust that we will be cared for. An overly self-sufficient person has not come to terms with his weakness, so he tries to hide his vulnerability by always appearing strong—by never needing others. Because it is based on a denial of weakness, this type of self-sufficiency is a false strength. Connection to others protects us from this misperception.

Allowing our true personality to come forth means exposing our innermost selves not only to others, but to ourselves as well. We are, all of us, understandably scared of the unknown within us: our suppressed memories and repressed emotions. In our psychological birth, the suppressed parts and hidden potential of our personality surface, revealing the full truth about ourselves. Something completely new emerges—something fresh and fragile.

A psychological birth is just as dramatic as a physical birth, during which the baby comes into the world after having his head and whole body squeeze through the birth canal. The event of birth is intense, and the newcomer's very survival may be at risk. In this first embrace of life, there are no guarantees but one: the baby cannot stay in the womb. He must leave it, heading toward the unknown.

This is the case in psychological birth as well, during which a person becomes a personality. A psychological birth can happen only after we acknowledge our weakness, making first contact with our vulnerability and helplessness. This profound experience challenges us to change, again offering only one assurance—that we will be loved.

survival strategies camouflage a lack of love

Without love, especially in childhood, our true personality cannot survive and flourish. What happens when our personality remains buried? We create survival strategies.

We may identify so strongly with our survival strategies that they become our new false self. Our true identity remains hidden from us as we carry our false identity with us into adulthood, reacting to people, events, and ourselves through this false self. We live a life bound by the past, more precisely, bound by the lack of love we experienced in the past.

Negative Individualism Is Isolating

A person who has not received the love he needed in order to develop and reach his full potential is trapped in a prison made up of his unmet needs. Unable to see others as they really are, he sees in them only what they can give to him. This leads to negative individualism: because he needs so much himself, he is unable to give—to himself, to his children, to anyone. A needy child may arouse hatred in a parent who needs what the child is asking for.

Negative individualism is becoming a psychological epidemic in our culture. With our sense of community crumbling, we have fewer chances to connect with others. As we become more isolated, the love we need so desperately becomes ever more scarce. The less love we have, the greater our inner deficit and the less we have to give others. This is why everybody is running around seeking self-fulfillment, when, in fact, they are looking for love.

Negative individualism is always founded on fear, feeling unsafe and uncourageous. We feel safe only when we are surrounded by love; if we lose love, we also lose our sense of safety. When we do have love in our lives, we learn to lean on others. If we are denied this crucial lesson, we must resort to the only support we feel we can count on: our own.

All this leads to isolation. If we have not had the opportunity to experience safety when interacting with loving and well-meaning people, we will not trust others. We do not allow anyone to get close to us—even if we live surrounded by crowds of people. In fact, we may use frenetic social activity to escape true closeness with others, surrounding ourselves with so many people we simply do not have the time to really get to know any one of them.

Positive Individualism Builds a Sense of Community

Negative individualism is not the only option to dealing with unmet childhood needs; we can also choose positive individualism. However, this requires the presence of love in our adult lives. Positive individualism is born when our deepest needs are fulfilled, when we become seen and heard as our true selves, when we receive attention and appreciation, when someone sees us as important and wants to be close to us. We begin to see ourselves in the way that others now see us. We learn to value ourselves and to acknowledge our feelings and needs. We live according to our true selves, and we are aware of our identity in a profound way.

Once we have received so much love and attention from another, we have something to give. We no longer need to see things only from our own viewpoint; we can take others into consideration. We become human beings who respect others as their own separate selves. However, none of this is possible while we are still bound by negative individualism. When caught in that mindset, we are incapable of seeing others as subjects; instead, we see them as objects. Positive individualism builds itself on a sense of community and interdependence; negative individualism builds itself only on survival strategies. Whereas the latter is created to survive love's absence, the former is born in love.

God is love

What is the origin of love? Why are we dependent on love? Why do we need love, and why do we have to pay so much attention to our needs? If lovelessness leads to toughness and strength, what's wrong with that? Aren't these good and useful qualities?

God is love. God created the universe. If these two statements hold true, they constitute the core of reality: The universe is an expression of a loving will. Life is not a mere coincidence or a peculiar whim in empty space. The world is not ruled by chaos and life is not senseless; instead, it has meaning. If the universe is indeed an expression of a loving will, this meaningfulness rests on the fact that God loves what He creates. In other words, God loves us and the world we live in. This makes love the power of creation and the deepest principle behind all forms of life.

Our need for love is an indication of our search for the truth about both ourselves and the world. When we seek love, we are seeking the true nature and structure of our being. And when we find love, we find inner peace.

God is not a distant, unapproachable, and absolute fact. God is the current of love within the universe. He does not merely exist,

He happens. God is dynamic, constantly on the move, involved in the process of creation.

This mystical stream of love is impossible to understand with our intellect. It might be compared to a cosmic nuclear reactor that channels the power of creation to the universe. It is a cosmic dynamo—a power that holds vast galaxies together and originates and maintains the movement in an atom's microscopic core. It is the gigantic pulse of the universe, and it also moves the human heart. Within us we have an inkling of this awesome power, which calls us to live in harmony with it.

All of humankind's true being is related to God's being. God is not merely a principle or power; God is a personality. Thus, the source of power at the core of the universe is a *personal power*. As human beings, we are also personalities and therefore intrinsically the same as God. The concept of personality originates in God. Humanity did not invent it; we did not create the concept and then project it onto God. Humans are personalities because God is a personality. We find our deepest nature only after we face the power that created us. Only in this love can we ourselves be born as personalities.

the Holy Spirit gives birth to our personality

Does all this talk about God and the current of love have any practical meaning, or is it just theological musings? To find out, we must examine the question "Who or what is the Holy Spirit?"

The Holy Ghost is often mentioned in connection with different charismatic or ecstatic phenomena. These include speaking in tongues, prophesying, mystical or divine healing, and so on.

At emotionally charged evangelical meetings, when ailing supplicants are prostrated by a healer's touch, it is often described as the work of the Holy Spirit. This a questionable claim. Such encounters offer an outlet for many kinds of emotional pain; although the discharge of suppressed emotional energy is undeniably powerful, it should not be uncritically accepted as the work of the Holy Spirit. These people have not necessarily been touched by the Holy Spirit; it is more likely that they are caught up in the throes of their past pain. We will not examine these phenomena in more detail in this context; they require a forum of their own. Instead, we will examine other aspects of the Holy Spirit—aspects that often go unnoticed but are more essential.

Through the Holy Spirit, love is manifested again: this time, in an individual person. Love becomes real to us. This does not mean merely grasping the concept of love—it means experiencing love, knowing with our entire being that we are loved. Through the Holy Spirit, love becomes relevant and alive, tangibly touching us. When we feel that we are loved, we have the courage to be more vulnerable and become what we most deeply are. Therefore, all human growth is actually the work of the Holy Spirit. Touched by such love, we start to live instead of merely surviving.

true "speaking in tongues" is speaking the language of love

We may ask, "Does love have any practical value to humanity?" Nothing is more practical in our everyday life than the need for love. Every human being yearns for love. Children seek it from their parents, spouses from each other, friends from one another, patients from doctors, clients from therapists, parishioners from pastors. Even prostitutes are sought for love. It is a universal thirst.

When we bring our true personalities forward, we begin speaking a language of love. Love communicates a deep respect for another person's uniqueness, the freedom to be who they really are, and our wish for what is best for them. With the help of this language we give our support to each other—and we also receive it in return. The more we become our true selves, the more love we are able to receive. The more love we are able to receive, the more deeply we are able to love.

Since God is the origin of love, we experience something of God when we are touched by love. Making love to one's spouse is experiencing God's love. We feel God's love in the caring and warmth of a skillful massage practitioner's hands. When we are seen and heard in therapy, we experience God's love. In a neighbor's cheerful greeting, we catch a glimpse of God's love. Each genuine interaction speaks the language of love and therefore strengthens our personalities.

This language of love is transmitted nonverbally; it is more about being loving than about words. Often, putting the language of love into words can kill it. One of the worst mistakes a therapist or counselor can make is to be more interested in imposing his theoretical or religious beliefs on a patient than in meeting the patient in loving and truthful interaction. When we grow spiritually, we learn to recognize the origin of love; we do not need to have it spelled out.

love is always truthful

Love and truth belong together; they never appear separately. Without love, the "truth" is actually cruelty. Bluntly confronting someone with "the truth" damages and destroys; this approach is never constructive. Telling the truth always involves caring for the other person. When we combine love with truth, we may condemn a person's wrongdoings, but the person remains certain that he is loved.

This is also the difference between shame and guilt. A sense of guilt signals that we have done wrong; when the wrongdoings are confessed, there is forgiveness. We do not lose our human dignity in the process. When we feel shame, we feel that not only have we done wrong, but that we *are* wrong, having no human dignity. Shame, a result of lovelessness, seeks to damage and destroy our personality, whereas love seeks to strengthen it. Love understands us, but condemns the evil in us. Love understands murderers, rapists, torturers, and thieves, but strives to open their eyes to the evil within them. This is truth with love. When love opens our eyes to our evil acts, we feel guilty. When we become aware of this guilt, we feel the need for mercy—which is a need for love. It is our desire to seek shelter from judgment.

Love leads us to continue to discover the truth about ourselves. The more love we receive, the better able we are to deal with our imperfection and incompleteness—the evil inside us.

Love and truth are gifts from the Holy Spirit, the Spirit of Truth. Truth reveals the falsehoods in us, our sins, removing any insincerity or fear that prevents us from birthing our true personality. This kind of truth never harms or insults us. It may hurt, but for the ultimate purpose of healing our being.

love awakens wounds

A person who has never received love does not know what he has never experienced. Lovelessness has become a normal state of being for him. He does not wonder at this, but accepts it as natural.

But when he encounters real love, he recognizes the lack of love he has always lived with. Love forms a new background against which this lack of love is revealed. Thus, love hurts the person who has been forced to do without it. Knowing this, we can understand why many people who are harboring internal wounds push away the loving overtures of others when they come too close.

Newfound love awakens the keen awareness of love's previous absence—both the lovelessness that someone has been subjected to and that which they may have caused. When we meet true love—for example, in a relationship or in therapy—we notice that what was called love in our childhood was not love after all, but more like cruelty disguised as love. Love now reveals how we have had to carry, often as shame, everything that our parents left unresolved. As mentioned earlier, when parents have not resolved their own pain and unfinished business, they pass their inability to love on to their children. This legacy destroys each generation's instinct to grow into their true and authentic selves. When love does appear at last, it awakens a person to his right to be whole and unique.

our wounds become our points of contact

Inner wounds, once revealed, bring people closer to each other because they lead to honest and open interaction. Our pain forms a true point of commonality between people. Only by acknowledging our mutual weakness can we get close to each other.

As mentioned earlier, strength does not elicit either affection or compassion. Strength is respected, feared, even envied, but it is not loved. But it is easy to love weakness. Weakness is utterly human; in it lies our true identity. That weakness makes us vulnerable is one of our best-kept secrets. When we see someone else's weakness, we identify with it; we recognize our own weakness—and our own humanity. This is the power of the compelling fictional characters we watch at the movies or read about in books; in their weaknesses and vulnerability, in their wounds revealed, we see ourselves.

There are those, of course, in whom the humanness of another person inspires contempt. These people are not yet ready to face their own human weakness. They run away from it, clinging to the illusion of their perfection. They see other people's weakness as a threat, a reminder of their own failings. These people cannot respond with compassion to someone else's weakness; instead, they try to take advantage of it. There is good reason to look out for these people, who do not possess the true capacity for closeness and honest interaction. There is no good reason to go and play the lamb among a pack of wolves.

love removes fear

Fear is always a companion to lovelessness. As mentioned earlier, fear arises from chronic insecurity. It is born when a human being cannot join others as a member of a loving and safe community. Cares, worries, and grief fill the life of a person who does not dare—or does not know how—to share his problems and concerns with others.

It is essential that people who are fearful are able to speak and be heard. This allows something wonderful to happen. When we speak about our concerns to somebody who listens and is really present, our burden decreases. Simply talking about a situation may not necessarily change it externally, but our attitude toward it changes. We regain our sense of proportion; we see our situation as less desperate. We are no longer immobilized by our problems, but see them as things that we can do something about. Our connection with another person vanquishes our fear and isolation.

When we know what it is to be supported and loved, we have the courage to stand alone. This is our seventh paradox: *Only together can we be alone.* We tolerate our separateness, facing our problems and taking responsibility for our own life. We gain this ability when we have received love and learned to join others without clinging or being overly dependent on them.

CHAPTER 8

if you seek eternity, live in the here and now

Through the ages, it seems we humans have harbored a desire for something beyond this life. We have always harbored a longing for something better, greater, more perfect, and more permanent—and we have never been content with the notion that death marks the end of everything, including our identity.

It's been said that we have religions because we die. Death is the great reminder, the great shocker and shaker. One day we will be no more; one day we will become what we once walked on: dirt.

What will be left of us when this has happened? Will anything be left of us? What happens to our identity when our body turns into dust? Will our identity continue to live in our soul? Or will we dissolve into atoms after having felt, thought, needed, given and taken, loved and hated, written poems, composed music, wondered, feared and dared, dreamed, and realized our dreams on this earth? Will the travelers of this earth disappear without a trace after having experienced a lifespan of joys and sorrows? Will only memories be left of us? If so, could we imagine anything more cruel? Who could be so fiendish as to create all these wondrous beings only to see them turn into dust? It is hard to imagine a greater lack of love.

So is there a God? If God exists, we can find something greater than death. For God is essentially about death.

But God is also about love: if God does not love, He may well let death be the end of everything, even though He is almighty in His power. But this would make Him a devastating power, who allows our identities to be destroyed, rather than a preserving power. This would make God evil, not loving.

But if God is love, as we have said earlier, then our lives have a purpose: we are presented with the opportunity of finding a meaningful life, and thus it makes a difference how we live our lives. We can find a direction, and we can live our lives with an awareness of being carried and guided by love.

no matter how hard we try, the sacred will not leave us alone

We live in a very secular culture, in which the commercial seems to have replaced the sacred: consuming has become larger than life. Insidiously, material goods have become the essence of life: we are what we own. Consuming has become a holy act. Stores and shopping malls, our modern temples, must therefore be open every day, even on Sundays.

What happens when nothing is revered as sacred? Have we excluded the sacred from our lives for good? Have we overturned all the values on which past generations based their culture—the values that gave their everyday lives a rhythm and a feeling of purpose? Have we managed to shift our focus completely to "all these things" and to quiet the questions and disturbing delusions about a hereafter? If we look on the surface of our modern lives, this certainly seems to be the case.

We humans have always longed for something greater than ourselves. For as long as we have had a consciousness, we have sought something beyond death, channeling this yearning into religion, art, mysticism, and communing with nature. We have always reached for the heavens, for the source of life and the defeat of death.

Do we still harbor this longing, or have cars, televisions, home espresso machines, camera phones, and gas grills satisfied our yearning so profoundly that we have found inner peace? When we look around us, the opposite appears to be true. Rest has become restlessness. Quiet has become disquiet. Presence and stillness have become constant hurry and chronic lack of time. We seem to be running faster and faster, and we have no time to stop and wonder where we are running and why.

We are running because we have lost our connection with our inner depth, with our true identity and our purpose for living. And so we run: life seems to have gotten away from us, and we must hurry after it. In so doing, we try to catch anything that even remotely resembles life: experiences, entertainment, the more the better. But the faster we run, the more life seems to elude us—it is as though we reach our hand into a fog, fervently trying to grab anything at random. The more life eludes us, the faster we have to run, and so we chase what we are fleeing from: our authentic self, our purpose. But we need not catch life; we could simply let life catch us—if we could just stop.

Does this mean that we have lost touch with our inner selves and our deeper connections for good? Has this loss benumbed our sense of the sacred? These questions occurred to me at a church service a while ago.

The church was full that Sunday. Many of the people did not usually attend church, but they had come to celebrate the confirmation of their children. Before the service, the priest mentioned that taking photographs was not allowed in the altar area during the Holy Communion and the confirmation. He needed to point this out to a church full of adults; apparently—and amazingly—this rule had not been respected on previous occasions. When the service began, it became clear that many of the congregation could not calm down and be present during the dignified celebration; they continued to adjust their cameras and video recorders. Instead of trying to be still and sense the solemn ambience, they tried to capture it on film, presumably to view later. They could not allow themselves to be touched by the sacred; rather, they tried to control it. Throughout the service, cell phones were ringing here and there, and people were chatting. The general feeling at the church was restlessness.

This made me wonder why we must be expressly reminded when something is sacred and should not be disturbed or disrupted. Have we abandoned the sacred to attend to more earthly needs? No, this has not happened: our ability to experience and long for the sacred continues to live in our restlessness, in our anxiety, distress, exhaustion, and confusion. Our yearning for the sacred lives on in our malaise, and the more we distance ourselves from the sacred, the worse we feel. So our cultural sickness is actually a sign of health: our hope lies in our hopelessness.

what is the meaning of the time between birth and death?

Everyone who has witnessed a loved one's dying knows he has witnessed something sacred; the presence of death never leaves us unmoved—it may shock us or render us silent, but it always leaves a mark on our soul. The same applies to birth: holding a newborn is like holding a miracle; we can sense an unexplainable holiness and intimations of eternity. All traces of cynicism disappear when we hold a miracle.

If we are present when a loved one dies or is born, we briefly sense an opening between here and the hereafter; for a moment, we feel the presence of something greater than this life.

What meaning do we apply to life, to the time between birth and death? The meaning depends on how we live our lives. Do we become so absorbed in our own concept of time that we lose the sense of life's temporariness? Or do we maintain a sense of eternity, recognizing that we are on a journey to somewhere beyond this time? Such a sense of eternity is a sense of grace—an awareness that life is a gift, not something we can earn or demand. We receive this gift because we are loved.

But how can we maintain this sense of eternity, this attitude of wonderment? How can we avoid cynicism and tired indifference? How can we learn not to take life for granted? As far as I can see, the Christian faith holds answers to these questions; the Christian faith holds something to which we should listen if we have lost our ability to wonder and taken time into our own hands. In essence, Christianity sends a message about what happened when time was placed in a new and surprising context—God's eternal love.

love is the source of all paradoxical wisdom

Love is God's reply to our bottomless cry for something beyond this life—a loving answer to the yearning for eternity that humankind has harbored through the ages.

Because we cannot reach God through our own effort, God reaches out for us; our part is to accept what we are now offered. It is not our struggle that matters, but rather our openness and receptiveness.

But what is this receptiveness? It is faith. Faith is the channel for love's entry into our time, our daily lives—not even Jesus was capable of working miracles when surrounded by unbelief. Miracles do not happen without faith; without faith, we are left at the mercy of our own capabilities or lack of capabilities. Without faith, there is no sense of eternity, a reality beyond this life; we are left with the laws of time. Without faith, there is only random, circumstantial love—the human kind, which can be hard to find. There is no great meaning or purpose—only that which is humanly sensible.

The core message of Christianity is that we are loved. God loves us. This a terrifying fact, for if it is true that this loving Person exists, then we must face all the untruth that still exists because we have not received the love that was always there for us. But before we can assess what is true and what is not, we first need to discover

if you seek eternity, live in the here and now

what is true within us. And so we must face our entire life—our psychological reality, our history. We must have the courage to face our skeletons, one after the other.

Every one of us has experienced a lack of love, in adulthood and in childhood. There is no such thing as a perfect childhood, because there are no perfect parents; there are no perfect parents, because there are no perfect people—there are only incomplete and imperfect people.

Because of this lack of love, having faith is difficult for every one of us, for to have faith means to have faith in love. We need this faith to believe that love is the greatest power in life—that this Great Power has taken the trouble to become flesh and bring the message of love to us. This love is within us; we can find that which is greatest in life inside of us.

Love Is within Us

God's love changes everything we knew, turns everything upside down. Thus, our ability to be confused and lost becomes more valuable than ready and certain answers. The ability to wonder now connects us with our inability to save ourselves. Love makes our journey our destination. Life is endless dynamic motion, development, change, relinquishment—letting go of the old to make space for something new.

We learned that strength does not lie in controlling others; true power can be found in weakness and in serving others. We find our strength when we humbly acknowledge and reveal our weakness.

God's love also means that faith becomes more important than religion—if religion is primarily a safe way for us to achieve goodness, then religion becomes useless and in fact is an obstacle to faith. Religion is faith misunderstood, a desperate effort to earn goodness. This type of religiousness is love's greatest enemy: after all, the good and the blameless were the ones who felt most threatened by Jesus, and it was they who nailed him to the cross. But love ends our pointless efforts to save ourselves; instead, it offers us the gift of salvation.

Love Waits Patiently

Because of love, our struggles have lost their power—no effort or achievement will earn us a good life. We can find a good life only if we stop and acknowledge our weakness and frailty. Growth is not about becoming better; it is about becoming more human, more open and receptive to love. Our goodness is not *our* goodness; it is goodness that we have been given; we cannot earn it through our own effort.

Because of love, our real strength lies not in our hurry and our endless imperative to perform, but in our ability to trust silently, in our ability to rest. Our ability to rest becomes the foundation of our effectiveness.

To find a good life, we need not become religious, moralistic, or impeccable, or otherwise act against our deepest nature. We need only to be open and receptive to the reality that we are loved.

God loves; God calls; God waits patiently.

Jesus could not step down from the cross, even though he was mockingly asked to do so. He demonstrated, on the cross, the true essence of love: love in the face of a seeming defeat. But this supposed defeat led to the greatest of victories: this love laid the foundation for Christianity, a movement that changed the history of humankind—a movement whose ultimate purpose and ultimate power is yet to be seen.

If you seek a sense of eternity, a reality beyond this life, live where eternity is present. Live in time; live in the here and now. Live in love.

index

A

Addiction, 40
Alcoholics Anonymous, 25–28
Alcoholism
  in author's childhood, 2–5
  fear of change and, 46
  as a safety structure, 39–40
  12-step program, 6, 25–28
Anger, 52, 114, 119
Augustine, Saint, 63
Authentic self. *See also* Personality; True identity
  connecting with, 43, 92–93, 106, 116
  heroes approaching, 50–54
  loss of, 67–68, 121, 138–139
  outward impressions versus, 18, 19
  revealing, 20–21, 58, 64–65
Autonomy, 109–111

B

Being, 86, 89–92
Birth to conscious life, 32–34, 125, 140
Bullies, 20
Bureaucracy, 48–49

C

Change, fear of, 45–46
Childhood
  inner images from, 49–50
  love lacking in, 22–23, 24, 41–43, 95, 126, 133–134
  unmet needs of, 110
  unresolved issues from, 111–115
Christianity, 36–37, 51, 140–141
Controlling life, 31–32, 34, 36–37, 40
Courage
  to face the truth, 53–54
  as fear turned into prayer, 46–47
  to give up hurriedness, 54–55
  to grow up, 49–50
  of heroes, 47, 58–59
  to rest and trust, 106
  to say "no," 122–123
Creativity, 44, 104, 106–107
Cynicism, 53

D

Dangerous life, 44, 45–46, 104, 122
Death
  heavenly kingdom and, 65
  as a reminder, 136–137
  sacredness of, 140
  seeking beyond, 138
  vanquishing, 14, 31
  viewed as weakness, 30
Deep life, 60, 67, 101–102
Dependency on others, 81–82
Disaster, 39–40, 56–57
Divorce, 5, 51
Dogma, 53
Dragon archetype, 50, 58
Dreams, 58, 104

E

Efficiency, 92, 105–108
Emotional well-being, 118–119
Emptiness, 68–69

Entertainment, 80–81
Enthusiasm, 65
Eternity, 140, 141, 144
Exhaustion/tiredness, 91–92

F

Faith
  as channel for love, 141
  defined, 48
  of heroes, 47–49, 53, 58–59
  importance of, 142–143
  living in, 64, 82
  religiousness replacing, 72
Fear, 44–47, 57, 135
Feelings, 52–53, 118–122
Femininity, 114–115
Freedom, 81–82, 118

G

God
  connecting with, 82, 105
  essence of, 86
  as love, 59, 123, 128–129, 131, 137, 141–142
  owning everything we have, 75–80
  as a personality, 129
  religion replacing, 36, 48
  trust in, 87–89, 105
Guilt, 72, 74, 76, 132

H

Heavenly kingdom
  loss of, 67–75
  meaning of, 62–65
  seeking, 65–66
Heroes
  approaching authentic self, 50–54
  courage to grow up, 49–50
  facing fear, 57
  faith and courage of, 47–49, 53, 58–59
  listening to dreams, 58
  loneliness of, 55–56
  refusing to rush, 54–55
Holy Spirit, 11, 129–130, 133
Honesty, emotional, 52–53
Hope, 25–28, 64, 65
Humility
  to accept our weakness, 21, 27
  for coping with wealth, 77
  described, 12, 18
  importance of, 8, 106
Hurriedness. *See also* Time
  as a choice, 23, 25, 73, 84–85, 97
  as disconnection from true identity, 138–139
  giving up, 54–55, 97
  lacking time to simply be, 86, 89
  learning to do less and achieve more, 92–93

I

Individualism, 126–128
Inner businessman, 78–80
Inner monk, 79–80
Institutions, 48–49
Intellect, 9–10, 12
Invisible, becoming, 39
Isolation, 126, 127
Issues, 102–103, 111–115, 116

J

Jesus
  demonstrating love, 143–144
  on healing the sick, 27

on the heavenly kingdom, 62, 63
on the Holy Spirit, 11
life of, 37
loneliness on the cross, 55–56
on materialism, 61–62, 67
miracles of, 141
refusal to be intimidated, 51
religiousness dismissed by, 62
sectarianism and, 36
teachings of, 10–11, 13
on truth, 93
on wealth, 77
Joy of work, 106–107

L

Language of love, 131–132
Living the life of others, 39–40
Loneliness, 55–56, 119
Love
  carrying us to safety, 34–35, 126–127
  childhood lacking, 22–23, 24, 41–43, 95, 126, 133–134
  as the deepest value, 70
  dependence on, 23, 81–82
  feeling worthy of, 86
  freedom needed for, 118
  God as, 59, 123, 128–129, 131, 137, 141–142
  heavenly kingdom of, 64
  Holy Spirit manifesting, 130
  inner wounds revealed through, 133–135
  Jesus demonstrating, 143–144
  lack of, 22–25, 42–43, 91, 142
  language of, 131–132
  need for, 21, 104, 128
  personality encouraged with, 109–110, 125, 131
  religiousness without, 87–88
  safety through, 34–35, 44, 126–127
  seeking for, 28–29, 123, 126
  truth told with, 21, 132–133
  within us, 142–143
  weakness fostered by, 19–20, 21
Loyalty, true, 52

M

Marriage
  autonomy in, 109–111
  mutual respect in, 116–117
  personal responsibility in, 118–119
  saying "no," 122–123
  sharing versus taking away pain, 119–122
  unresolved issues affect on, 111–115
Materialism, 35, 60, 61–62, 67, 137
Mercy, 132
Miracles, 141
Money, 70, 74–75, 77
Monroe, Marilyn, 68
Morals, 72

N

Negative individualism, 126–127, 128
Niceness, chronic, 36–37, 52

P

Pain and suffering, 94, 100–101, 117, 120–122
Paradox, 10–11, 12–13
Parents, 50, 72–73, 74, 81
Past, facing, 116–117

Perfection, seeking, 38–39
Personal growth
  becoming receptive to love, 143
  choosing, 97–99
  facing the past, 116–117
  humility essential to, 8
  risk of being rejected for, 99–102
Personality. *See also* Authentic self
  birth of, 103–104
  described, 93
  encouraged through love, 109–110, 125, 131
  gift of, 87
  God as, 129
  hidden, 126
  revealing, 103
  shame-bound, 95
Positive individualism, 127–128
Postponing life, 37–38
Power, 18, 71, 74, 75
Prayer, 46–47, 57
Presley, Elvis, 68
Prince archetype, 49–50
Psychological birth, 125

R

Rejection, 99–102, 119
Religion, 36, 48, 142–143
Religiousness, 51, 62, 72, 87–89
Respect, 116–117
Responsibility
  for feelings, 119–122
  saying "no," 122–123
  taking, 116–117, 118–120
  for use of time, 98–99
Restfulness, 93, 105–106, 107–108
Risk, 37, 44, 99–102

S

The sacred, 137–140
Safety
  in birth to conscious life, 32–34
  love providing, 34–35, 44, 126–127
  self-made structures for, 35–40, 45–46
  through controlling life, 31–32, 34
Science, 35–36
Sectarianism, 36
Self-conceit, 37
Self-sufficiency, unhealthy, 68, 81, 87, 124–125
Sex, 71, 74, 75–76
Shame
  in author's childhood, 3–4
  guilt versus, 132
  lack of love manifesting as, 22–25, 42
  personality bound with, 95
Silence
  choosing, 53, 54–55
  inner issues uncovered in, 102–103
  journey begins with, 15
  listening to, 103–104
  strength in, 105
Soul, 67, 85, 90
Speaking in tongues, 130, 131
Strength
  defining, 16–17
  false, 20–21, 88, 125
  found in weakness, 8, 17–19
  in quietness and trust, 105
  unhealthy (sick), 4, 16, 18
Substance abuse, 40, 71, 74
Success, 60–61, 67–68, 76–77, 96
Survival strategies, 126–128

T

Technology, 83–84
Therapy, 94
Time. *See also* Hurriedness
  lack of, 54–55, 83–86
  living in the present, 83, 97
  taking responsibility for, 98–99
Tiredness/exhaustion, 91–92
Tranquility, 54–55
Tranströmer, Tomas, 13
True identity. *See also* Authentic self
  disconnection from, 126, 138
  finding, 20–21, 22, 23–24, 64–65, 123
Trust, 87–89, 105, 106
Truth
  courage to face, 53–54
  false strength revealed by, 20–21
  as gift from Holy Spirit, 133
  knowing who we are, 93–94
  revealed through paradox, 10–11
  told with love, 121, 132–133
12-step program, 6, 25–28

V

Values
  deepening, 96
  learning through weakness, 28–30
  superficial, 70–71, 72–73, 85–86, 90
Van Gogh, Vincent, 47–48
Vulnerability, 52–53, 69–70, 125

W

Weakness
  acknowledging, 8, 20–21, 26–27, 134
  contempt for, 16–17, 20, 134–135
  hiding and denying, 21, 27–28, 125
  learning values through, 28–30
  love fostering, 19–20, 21
  strength found in, 8, 17–19
Wealth, 18, 61–62, 71, 77
Wisdom, 12–13
Work, joy of, 106–107
Workplace, 52, 90, 99–101
Worthiness, 41, 86, 90

ABOUT THE AUTHOR

Tommy Hellsten is a therapist with over thirty years of experience and an author whose books have sold more than 400,000 copies in Europe. In his native Finland, he is often referred to as the country's national therapist.

A pioneer in the treatment of emotional problems related to codependency and substance abuse, Hellsten instigated the national network of self-help groups for adult children of alcoholics in Finland. His first book, *Hippo in the Living Room*, introduced the concept of codependency to Finland in 1991. Sales of *Hippo in the Living Room* broke the previous record for a self-help book; it has been in print ever since, and the twenty-ninth edition was published in summer 2007.

Hellsten's work as a counselor, writer, speaker, and consultant is based on a synthesis of psychoanalytical thought, Christianity, and the 12-step program. Above all, however, he draws on his own life experience. He regards his training at Hazelden in Minnesota and the Caron Foundation in Pennsylvania as the most significant influences in his professional life.

Hellsten holds a master's degree in theology from the University of Helsinki. He is married and has three adult children from a previous marriage. In addition to maintaining an active therapeutic practice, he has established a four-year training program for those in the helping professions on how to meet their clients as people rather than as patients.